Assessing Critical Skills

Jon Mueller

Professional Development Resources for K–12
Library Media and Technology Specialists

To my wife, Rita

Library of Congress Cataloging-in-Publication Data

Mueller, Jon.
  Assessing critical skills / Jon Mueller.
    p. cm.
  Includes bibliographical references and index.
  ISBN-13: 978-1-58683-282-7 (pbk.)
  ISBN-10: 1-58683-282-4 (pbk.)
  1. Educational tests and measurements. I. Title.
  LB3051.M847 2008
  371.26--dc22

                              2008019609

Cynthia Anderson: Editor
Carol Simpson: Editorial Director
Judi Repman: Consulting Editor

Published by Linworth Publishing, Inc.
3650 Olentangy River Road
Suite 250
Columbus, Ohio 43214

ISBN 13: 978-1-58683-282-7
ISBN 10: 1-58683-282-4

Mixed Sources
Product group from well-managed
forests and other controlled sources
www.fsc.org Cert no. SW-COC-002283
© 1996 Forest Stewardship Council

5 4 3 2 1

Table of Contents

Table of Figures

About the Author

Dr. Jon Mueller is Professor of Psychology at North Central College in Naperville, Illinois. Along with teaching and writing about assessment, Jon consults on the development of standards and assessments at the K-12 and post-secondary levels. He is particularly interested in the teaching and assessing of information literacy, scientific thinking, and other skill development. Jon is the author of the popular and award-winning online text, *Authentic Assessment Toolbox*, at <http://jonathan.mueller.faculty.noctrl.edu/toolbox>.

Introduction

I have been teaching an introductory psychology course at North Central College for more than 20 years. Most of the students in the course are freshmen, and many of them struggle; I give out more Ds and Fs than I would like. Some wrestle with extracting meaning out of the reading, some struggle with writing, some are not able to prepare effectively for a challenging exam. Many students struggle with more than one of these tasks. Unfortunately, I am not the only teacher with this experience.

Some of the freshmen are wise enough to talk to me about their difficulties. I learn about their weak study strategies, questionable time-management choices, and poor note-taking skills. As I reflect upon why students have such difficulty in an entry-level college course, I cannot remember ever thinking, "If only they had learned more about history, or had taken more math, or more psychology, they would not be struggling so much in my course." Instead, I notice that those who put in some effort and still perform poorly cannot write very well, do not ask questions when they are confused, have difficulty reading a textbook, do not take very good notes or outline them well, cannot think critically about evidence and claims, and cannot judge when they are having difficulty with any of these tasks. It is not surprising they struggle. More ominous is the fact that the same skills students are struggling to exhibit in my course—read, explain, persuade, analyze, self-correct, summarize, collaborate—are the very skills that will be most critical to their success throughout college, work, and life.

Yes, I am playing the game of pawning off some of my failure on those educators who taught these students before me. However, our failure to teach the skills most critical to students' success in school and beyond is endemic to the entire K-16 educational system in the United States. We ask students to memorize reams of information that they will rarely if ever use again, but fail to adequately teach them the knowledge and skills they will need to meet the daily challenges of their lives. How do I know if I should try this product? How can I persuade others to follow my lead? How can I tell if this is a reliable source? How would I know if I am applying this information effectively or accurately? How do I know when I am done with this task?

As with most significant problems, there is not one explanation for why many students fail to acquire these skills, and there is no magic pill to fix it. We simply need to begin by recognizing how critical these skills are to success in school, in work, and in virtually every facet of life. We need to target skills such as information literacy, critical thinking, problem-solving, self-assessment and self-regulation, and learning how to learn as central goals of our educational efforts. When we identify something as a central goal, or standard, or outcome, we must determine if students are meeting these goals. We need to measure students' aptitude at displaying or applying these skills.

I recognize that we have failed our educators as well. Many have not been adequately trained in assessment in our teacher education programs or in faculty development efforts on the job. Consequently, most educators struggle enough with the assessment of student acquisition of the content of their disciplines; assessing something less tangible like critical-thinking skills or metacognitive skills is even more challenging.

How do you test for monitoring one's own progress or thinking critically or considering the perspective of others? We are not accustomed to trying to capture such performance. Yet, if we want educators to truly develop these skills in their students, educators need to become proficient at measuring student growth in these skills and then "closing the loop" by reviewing the data to determine better methods of instruction. That should take place within a school-wide effort to include all the educators from the classroom teacher to the librarian to the reading specialist.

It is a difficult task, but not an impossible one. It certainly is a necessary one, I believe. As W. James Popham (1999) so eloquently explains in his essay, "Why standardized tests don't measure educational quality," external tests are not the answer. They are not very effective indicators of whether or not students have benefited from the instruction in our classrooms. If I want to know if my students have become better thinkers in my class, I need to develop assessments tied directly to my instruction and my goals.

Thus, I believe there is a very pressing need for the assessment knowledge and skills I will walk readers through in this text. I will begin in Chapter 1 by arguing that far too much time and attention is given to the dissemination of soon-to-be-forgotten and rarely-used information at the expense of fostering the development of these critical skills. In Chapters 2 and 3 I will describe the critical skills in more detail. In Chapters 4 and 5 I will elaborate on the authentic assessment process to illustrate how the design of meaningful assessment of such skills can guide effective instruction of them. From that foundation, I will provide concrete examples and guidance in Chapters 6 through 9 on how to construct assessments for specific skills. Unfortunately, any such skill development that currently exists is not being delivered systematically. Thus, in Chapter 10, I will lay out a sample plan a school or district could adopt for a more coherent strategy to address the instruction and assessment of the critical skills.

Finally, recognizing that this may be new or at least overwhelming to consider on top of everything else educators (from classroom teachers to librarians) must face, I will suggest simple ways to get started on the task of assessing critical skills.

What Do Students Need To Succeed?

1

Ask yourself: How many times this week have you had the need to compute a cosine? Really? That many times? Okay, probably not.

Now ask yourself: How many times this week have you stopped to reflect upon a course of action you have taken to determine whether it was working, so that you could make adjustments as needed? Probably quite a few times. For example, if you are a teacher, and you taught today, you probably asked yourself "Did this work?" on more than one occasion. Were you then able to identify how to adjust your approach the next time if necessary?

In school, were you ever deliberately taught how to monitor such progress, evaluate your performance, and correct your errors? I am guessing you received at least as much direct instruction on computing a cosine as you did on these metacognitive skills. And, yet, I am guessing you likely needed to use the metacognitive skills hundreds of times more than you ever need to compute a cosine after you left school.

Ask yourself: How many times this week have you had the need to know the difference between an ionic bond and a covalent bond? Then ask yourself: How many times this week have you needed to evaluate the quality or relevancy of information you have come across?

Perhaps you actually did receive more instruction and practice on the skill of evaluating information than on types of chemical bonds, but was the amount of instruction in proportion to the degree with which you use those two concepts now?

"SCHOOLS ALREADY TEACH TOO MUCH"

In the U.S. school systems, students are asked to learn and recall an enormous amount of information: Names, dates, concepts, principles, and processes. How much did you have to memorize? How much of it do you remember? More importantly, how much of it do you use?

We give far too much attention to teaching information our students will rarely, if ever, use, and not nearly enough focus on essential skills they will apply on a daily basis. When did you last need to recall the capital of New

Hampshire, or the difference between anthropomorphism and personification, or how to graph a parabolic function? We do not know what information we will need in the future; much of it has yet to be created. Thus, it is far more important that we learn how to find the information we will need, make sense of it, evaluate it, summarize it, and communicate it than it is to acquire huge stores of information in memory, much of it never to be used again.

More than 20 years ago Gary Galles (1987) wrote an essay entitled, "Schools already teach too much" in which he makes the point others have made before and since:

> One expert after another finds students woefully ignorant in his or her field, then issues an urgent call for schools to teach more of it—more cultural literacy, more great books, more mathematics, science and computers, more history and humanities. Before we answer the reformers' calls by trying to fit more everything into school curricula, perhaps we should question their assumption that students will learn more if they are just taught more. The opposite may well be true.

In fact, a few years later, Frank Dempster (1993) reviewed the literature and answered that question in an article entitled "Exposing our students to less should help them learn more." Dempster presented compelling evidence that our curricula are "overstuffed and undernourished." Overstuffing our curricula inhibits the very processes research has found will promote substantial and sustained learning. For example, trying to teach too many topics lessens the opportunities to distribute learning over time for multiple exposures and multiple testing which strengthens recall (Bahrick & Hall, 2005; Dempster, 1989; Pashler, Zarow, & Triplette, 2003; Roediger & Karpicke, 2006). Furthermore, as Dempster notes, "... distributed practice does more than simply increase the amount learned; it frequently shifts the learner's attention away from the verbatim details of the material being studied to its deeper conceptual structure (p. 435)."

Similarly, opportunities for thoughtful reflection of ideas and concepts enhance their long-term retrieval (Willingham, 2003). Research has also found that the greater the number of topics taught the greater the chance for interference, which also significantly reduces retention (Dempster, 1993). On the other hand, time given to more practice with information tends to diminish the impact of interference (Campbell & Graham, 1985; Dempster, 1988).

Superficially addressing many topics also reduces the likelihood for transfer of learning to other contexts (Bereiter, 1995; Mayer & Wittrock, 1996; Pressley & Yokoi, 1994). Additionally, giving limited attention to a large number of facts and concepts prevents the necessary construction of meaning that each student must engage in for deep learning (Bransford & Vye, 1989; Forman & Kuschner, 1977; Neisser, 1967; Steffe & Gale, 1995; Wittrock, 1991).

Finally, research has found that cramming curricula with innumerable topics limits the opportunity to learn metacognitive strategies which have been found to enhance the learning of those topics (e.g., Alexander, Graham, & Harris, 1998; Hattie et al., 1996).

Dempster (1993), as have others, attributes some of our mile-wide, inch-deep curricula to the overstuffed textbooks we use. As Schmidt, McKnight and Raizen (1996) found in reviewing textbook data collected as part of the Trends in International Mathematics and Science Study (TIMSS), "U.S. mathematics textbooks designed for fourth and eighth graders cover an average of 30 to 35 topics, while those in Germany and Japan average 20 and 10 respectively for these populations. . . . The average U.S. science textbook at the fourth, eighth, and twelfth grade has between 50 and 65 topics; by contrast Japan has five to 15 and Germany has just seven topics in its eighth grade science textbooks (p. 5)." They add, "This preoccupation with breadth rather than depth, with quantity rather than quality, probably affects how well U.S. students perform in relation to their counterparts in other countries (p. 2)." In other words, even if all the facts and concepts we were teaching and that are stuffed into our textbooks were essential, the sheer volume of them overwhelms any chance students have of remembering much of it for longer than the two weeks leading up to an exam.

QUALITY OVER QUANTITY

There have been some efforts to reduce the staggering number of concepts and facts we teach students in this country. For example, the standards movement has attempted to streamline the curriculum by identifying only the most essential knowledge and skills to prepare students to become productive citizens (Schmoker & Marzano, 1999). Instead of using overstuffed textbooks to guide curriculum development, the idea has been to identify what is truly necessary for students to learn to be successful in school, work, and life and write that knowledge and skills into standards which will guide curricular and instructional development.

However, along the way many standards committees have gotten away from that goal and written exhaustive lists to satisfy all constituencies (Schmoker & Marzano, 1999). Thus, efforts to reduce the amount of material taught to the most essential get overrun by a desire to be inclusive of the priorities of all quarters. As Schmidt et al. noted,

> Reforms have already been proposed by political, business, educational and other leaders. Extensive efforts are underway to implement these standards, but the implementation process itself is shaped by the prevailing culture of inclusion. Like the

developers of curricula and the publishers of textbooks, teachers add reform ideas to their pedagogical quivers without asking what should be taken away (Schmidt et al., 1996, p. 4).

Consequently, a sort of tragedy of the commons emerges. That is, as each constituency seeks to improve the final document by adding more to it, ironically, the collective value is significantly reduced.

Even when standards writers have been more judicious in crafting an essential list of knowledge and skills, they do not sufficiently address the question: "How much of it do we actually use?" Instead of asking, "What knowledge and skills are most important to the future of our children?" too often the guiding question for writing standards has been "What topics are most important to the field?"

Just as streamlining the standards frequently has been thrown off course by good intentions, another laudable goal of many educators, reformers, and politicians—a push for increased rigor in our standards and curricula—has sometimes met a similar fate. Challenging students with higher standards and greater expectations tends to increase their performance (Kuklinski & Weinstein, 2001; Rosenthal, 2002). However, the push for increased rigor has often led to a push for more unnecessary content. Calls for rigor have often been linked to calls for increased accountability which has often been linked to increased standardized testing, as in the case of No Child Left Behind (NCLB).

One unsettling consequence of increased standardized testing has been an emphasis on teaching and testing content. Multiple-choice tests do not easily lend themselves to the effective assessment of critical skills such as effective collaboration, information seeking and evaluation, or monitoring one's own progress. Such tests are better at measuring whether or not a body of knowledge has been acquired (Haladyna, 1999). Thus, a lot of time has been expended on memorization of facts and preparation for standardized testing. More significantly, devoting so much focus to the considerable volume of names, dates, concepts, principles, and processes reduces the likelihood that we will teach students what is even more critical for them to learn.

WHAT DO STUDENTS NEED TO SUCCEED?

As I write this chapter, another report comes out about the lack of knowledge in Americans. Significantly more Americans can name Homer's son on The Simpsons than name one of Homer's epic poems about ancient Greece. We are better at remembering the names of the seven dwarves than the names of the Supreme Court justices. Only 40% of us knew that Mercury was the closest planet to the sun (Zogby International poll, 2006).

Are you alarmed by this? Possessing knowledge about our social, political, and natural world is essential. Yet given the amount of information crammed into our heads it is not surprising that we have forgotten a great deal of it, particularly information that is rarely if ever needed. When did you last have occasion to use your knowledge of Mercury?

What is more disturbing is what we are not teaching. We are not teaching students much of the knowledge and skills that prepare them for the actual problems and challenges they will regularly face in school, work, and life. Students need to see that the curriculum connects to their lives and their futures. Given the failure of the current curriculum to consistently do so, school is not seen as relevant to many of our students. As a recent study noted, lack of relevance is one of the factors that leads to a significant number of students dropping out (Bridgeland, DiIulio, & Morison, 2006).

Regarding knowledge, we need to more carefully target the information students will truly require in their many roles within and beyond school. We must ask "What do homeowners, parents, employees, managers, citizens, travelers, community members need to know?" as guiding questions in designing standards and curricula.

More significantly, we must target the critical skills that will be even more essential for our students in school, work, and life. We are constantly called upon to solve problems, communicate clearly and persuasively, and collaborate successfully with others. Our success is critically dependent upon our being able to do so.

What are these skills? In the following chapter I will articulate a detailed set of critical skills that we as adults call upon continuously, across various contexts and roles, to help us succeed in school, work, and life. Then, in Chapter 3, we will examine how these skills are essential to success.

The Critical Skills Students Need

2

Why do I keep calling these "critical" skills? I use the term "critical" here, and in the title of the book, in two ways. First, I believe the skills I mentioned in Chapter 1, and that I will describe in more detail in this chapter, are essential to one's ability to function effectively and fully in our world: school, work, and life. I will make the case further in this chapter that possessing these skills (and having the disposition to apply them) will enable us to tackle problems across multiple and varied contexts, as well as best utilize the knowledge we have acquired.

Second, I call these skills critical because I believe they require or emphasize *critical thinking*. One cannot be a good communicator, good problem-solver, good collaborator, or good information seeker without careful and thoughtful participation in those processes.

It would be quite presumptuous of me to claim that I know what all the most critical skills are. So, I will simply argue that these are *some* of the most critical skills we need to succeed. Others could add to (and subtract from) this list. Yet, I am comfortable suggesting that those individuals who possess the skills described in the following list will be well prepared for most challenges they encounter. If that is true, should not teaching and assessing these skills be a central aspect of what we do in school?

"THE" CRITICAL SKILLS

In attacking a task such as generating a list of critical skills, it is helpful to try and categorize the items in the list. This gives more meaning to the items by highlighting similarities and differences. So, I have grouped a number of skills along four dimensions:

1) Skills related to interacting with others in the world
2) Skills related to thinking about the world
3) Skills related to adapting to the world
4) Skills related to solving problems in the world

INTERACTING WITH OTHERS

Since we are a social species, effectively interacting with other humans is often critical to our success. Thus, it is quite beneficial to be competent at:

- Communication Skills—including the abilities to read, write, speak, and listen in a particular language as well as in other common languages; express oneself through and interpret nonverbal communication; communicate through and interpret artistic expression
- Collaborative Skills—including the abilities to contribute to group activities and discussions; consider the ideas and perspectives of others; include others in the collaborative process; stay focused on the task; provide and receive feedback constructively
- Leadership Skills—including the abilities to model appropriate behavior; direct and organize the behavior of others; persuade others; manage conflict; take action and accept responsibility for the consequences
- Interpersonal Skills—including the abilities to take the perspective of others; manage conflict; manage one's emotions and impulses across a variety of interpersonal situations; maintain positive relations with others; adhere to appropriate boundaries when interacting with others

MAKING SENSE OF THE WORLD

Also, part of human nature is our capacity to reason and reflect upon the decisions and problems we encounter. Thus, the cognitive processes that often direct our behavior are also critical to our success. Such skills include:

- Logic or Reasoning Skills—including the abilities to draw appropriate inferences; deduce logical conclusions; identify assumptions; generate predictions; recognize faulty logic
- Quantitative Reasoning Skills—including the abilities to estimate; exhibit a sense of scale; interpret quantitative data in varied formats; use quantitative data to support arguments; interpret probabilities; recognize misuses of data
- Analytical Skills—including the abilities to identify patterns; identify the components of a concept or problem; identify appropriate criteria for judging a product or idea; compare and contrast concepts or processes; classify or organize elements along specified criteria
- Evaluation Skills—including the abilities to evaluate the validity of claims; evaluate the relevance of different types and sources of evidence for different types of claims or questions; evaluate the sufficiency of evidence to draw a conclusion; apply criteria to the judgment of a product or idea; identify possible errors and biases in

claims or conclusions
- Integration Skills—including the abilities to find connections between similar and dissimilar concepts or processes; combine disparate ideas into a new, coherent idea; synthesize a variety of components into a new product

PERSONAL GROWTH AND DEVELOPMENT

With such a plastic brain, humans have considerable capacity to adapt to the environment. The more we learn from our successes and failures and learn how to adjust accordingly the more successful we tend to be. That places considerable importance upon the following skills:

- Self-assessment Skills—including the abilities to apply relevant criteria to own work; identify strengths and weaknesses; judge when one has successfully completed a task
- Goal-setting Skills—including the abilities to identify clear goals; identify realistic goals; identify goals relevant to the task; identify effective responses to positive and negative outcomes
- Self-management Skills—including the abilities to manage one's time; be prepared; develop and follow successful routines; organize and plan appropriately; prioritize; respond flexibly to new situations; manage stress and handle distractions; act independently when necessary or appropriate
- Metacognitive Skills—including the abilities to monitor one's progress on a task; assess task difficulty; anticipate likelihood of difficulty on a task; acknowledge one's strengths and limitations; evaluate effectiveness of current and alternative strategies; recognize when a change in approach is needed and make adjustments; identify errors; take control of learning
- Study (or Learning) Skills—including the abilities to manage time for a task or situation; recognize the best strategies for certain kinds of tasks; outline or organize information to be learned; give meaning to the information to be learned; attach useful cues to the information to be learned; exhibit active engagement with information to be learned; make information personally relevant; use others wisely in service of learning of information; apply meta-memory knowledge to learning of information

SOLVING PROBLEMS

Virtually everything humans do can be thought of as a problem to be solved, a question to be answered, or a task to be completed. Thus, our success in life also depends upon developing skills which enhance our capacity to successfully approach, analyze, and complete tasks. Such skills include:

- Problem-solving Skills—including the abilities to identify a (the) problem; determine knowledge and skills necessary or helpful to solve the problem or complete the task; apply appropriate knowledge, rules and strategies to the problem; generate possible solutions; evaluate the feasibility and effectiveness of possible solutions; given relevant constraints, determine best possible solution(s)
- Information Literacy Skills—including the abilities to identify or frame a question to be answered; locate appropriate sources of information that address the question; access the information from a variety of sources; evaluate the accuracy, relevancy, authority, and currency of the information for the question; determine when sufficient information has been acquired to answer the question
- Creative or Innovative Skills—including the abilities to identify novel connections between disparate concepts and contexts; identify novel approaches to a process or task; combine disparate concepts, processes or tools in novel ways
- Technical Skills—including the abilities to recognize appropriate tool(s) for specific tasks; contribute to the completion of a task through effective application of tools

Note: I have not listed dispositions or habits of mind among these critical skills. Yet, research finds that those are critical as well. Someone might possess good critical-thinking skills, but if she is not disposed to applying them in certain situations or in general those skills are not employed (Bensley, 2006; Perkins, Jay, & Tishman, 1993). However, to keep attention here on how to develop these skills, that discussion will be left to others.

Okay, take a look at the list of skills. Obviously, these skills overlap considerably within and between the categories. Also, one could choose a variety of names that capture their focus, but this categorization helps elucidate the relevance and importance of these skills. Given that, what do you see when you look at the list?

When scanning the list and imagining a student employing most or even many of these skills, can you understand a teacher's enthusiasm for working with such a student? When you imagine an employee (or supervisor) or colleague or neighbor or leader with such skills do you see great promise for such a person in any sphere of life? These are skills we can teach, beginning at an early age. We just are not doing it now, at least not systematically and not for most students.

BEYOND READING, 'RITING, AND 'RITHMETIC

A few critical skills, such as reading and writing, do receive considerable attention in our schools. Yet, even there, in part because of our overstuffed curricula, many students do not receive sufficient instruction and practice in how to read the variety of nonfiction texts they will encounter in school and beyond. Similarly, too many students graduate high school with weak communication skills.

Other critical skills, such as

- information literacy skills
- metacognitive strategies
- problem-solving skills
- collaborative skills

receive far less attention, particularly relative to the frequency with which we are called upon to use them in numerous contexts.

I am not referring to discipline-specific skills—how to conduct scientific inquiry, how to multiply fractions, or how to converse in another language. Many of those are important as well. Rather, I am arguing for greater attention to those skills that cross all disciplines and thus do not belong to any one discipline. Given that most of these skills do not have a particular disciplinary home, they often receive much less attention even though they are often applied across a much greater range of contexts.

To explore these critical skills further, let us examine their *relevance* to school, work, and life.

Critical Skills for School, Work, and Life

3

CRITICAL SKILLS STUDENTS NEED IN SCHOOL

As a middle-school educator, imagine you could have one of the following two students coming to you from elementary school. One student miraculously has retained every fact or piece of knowledge he ever learned in school. However, that student comes to you with no thinking skills, no ability to reason, no study skills, and no metacognitive skills. The other student, just as miraculously, has gone through elementary school without retaining any fact or concept (okay, maybe this does not seem as miraculous), but she can think, reason, self-assess, and apply effective study skills. Whom would you prefer joining your class? Acknowledging that this is an absurd and very false dichotomy, educators invariably say they would prefer the latter student. Teachers and librarians have seen that the process of learning will be much more productive with students who can manage their own thinking and know how to learn.

Ask high-school teachers the same question about middle-school students coming to their school and you will likely get the same response. Educators in higher education also respond the same. We recognize the superior value of these critical skills. Furthermore, it illustrates that teachers recognize these skills are also necessary for future learning. We cannot teach students all the information they will need in the years to come, but we can teach them the skills to:

- effectively make sense of that information
- intelligently evaluate and choose among it
- comfortably adapt to it

Those students who are weaker in these skills are particularly likely to struggle in school. In an article entitled, "Why people fail to recognize their own incompetence," Dunning et al. (2003) review some research comparing stronger and weaker students. They conclude that the weaker students are "doubly cursed: Their lack of skill deprives them not only of the ability to produce correct responses, but also of the expertise necessary to surmise that they are not producing them." In fact, they are triply cursed: These students also tend to be less able to correct their errors even if they could recognize them. As Dunning et al. report, weaker students often fail to recognize which questions on a test they are getting right and which they are getting wrong (Sinkavich, 1995). How can they or why would they correct their answers if they do not appear wrong in the first place? Similarly, poor readers fail to recognize when they do not comprehend text they are reading (Maki & Berry, 1984). How would they know what to go back and re-read, or even when to do so?

Consider how often these skills are critical in an educational setting. Which would be a greater predictor of a student's success in school—the ability to recall the battles of the Revolutionary War or the ability to recognize when something one has read makes little sense or needs further examination? Which would be more useful in a work setting? Why are we not devoting significant attention to teaching these critical skills?

CRITICAL SKILLS WE NEED AT WORK

It would be interesting to ask an employer a comparable question: Imagine you could have one of the following two applicants for a position. One applicant possesses all of the job-specific knowledge that is required for that position, but that applicant is limited in his ability to:

- think critically
- find and evaluate information related to the job
- communicate effectively in that position
- problem solve on the fly
- monitor his own progress and make adjustments when needed

The other applicant possesses only limited job-specific knowledge but has mastered all of the skills just described. Which applicant would you be more likely to hire? If forced to choose between the two would not many employers prefer the latter applicant?

We learn much of the work-specific knowledge and skills on the job, through training, modeling, or experience. Thus, employers regularly report that what they seek from employees are the general skills that are critical to most work settings. For example, according to the *Greater Expectations National Panel Report* (2002), "business leaders seek graduates who can think analytically, communicate effectively, and solve problems in collaboration with diverse colleagues, clients or customers (p. ix)." Along with a deep understanding of the world around them and a sense of responsibility, the *Report* concludes that future workers need to be "empowered learners." That is, they "should learn to":

- Effectively communicate orally, visually, in writing, and in a second language

- Understand and employ quantitative and qualitative analysis to solve problems
- Interpret and evaluate information from a variety of sources
- Understand and work within complex systems and with diverse groups
- Demonstrate intellectual agility and the ability to manage change
- Transform information into knowledge and knowledge into judgment and action (p. xi)

Similarly, Karoly and Panis (2004), in a study of the "forces shaping the future workforce and workplace in the United States," found that "knowledge workers require high-level cognitive skills for managing, interpreting, validating, transforming, communicating, and acting on information. Valued skills include such non-routine analytic skills as abstract reasoning, problem-solving, communication, and collaboration (p. 201)." These same points are echoed in the *Partnership for 21st Century Skills Report*, "Results that matter: 21st century skills and high school reform (2006)." As the report notes, "Employers, educators and policymakers agree that the skills necessary for entering postsecondary education today are virtually the same skills necessary for success in the modern workplace (p. 11)."

If we ask what skill sets are common to most jobs, what skills you apply on a frequent basis in your work, we would likely identify a set of skills that include:

- communication
- collaboration
- problem-solving
- information literacy
- metacognition
- quantitative reasoning
- critical-thinking and reasoning skills

How much deliberate and focused attention and practice do these skills really receive in school? How many of our students are truly proficient in them when they graduate from college, much less from high school?

CRITICAL SKILLS FOR . . . LIFE

The term "life" here serves as a catch-all for all the other contexts or roles in which we find ourselves. Beyond being students and workers, many of our students will be parents and spouses, citizens and neighbors, homeowners and apartment dwellers, consumers and producers.

As parents, for example, we continually need to "outwit, outplay, outlast" our children. It has required us to be lifelong learners, to reassess constantly our goals, our strengths and weaknesses, our actions, our planning, and our values, to solve problems, to communicate clearly and persuasively, to listen well. How well prepared were you for those challenges?

Similarly, as new homeowners, much of the knowledge and skill we needed we lacked going into homeownership. We learned it on the "job." As mentioned earlier, there would have been more useful information and skills we could have learned in school that would have better prepared us to be a homeowner or apartment dweller. Of course, we might have forgotten much of it by the time we could afford our own place. That is another benefit of focusing attention in school on pervasive, critical skills. Once you have learned a skill well, and have many opportunities to practice it because it is so frequently required, you are much less likely to lose that ability than you are to forget facts you once memorized.

Citizens are often asked to consider proposals from politicians, community leaders, and fellow citizens. Are we well equipped to evaluate critically the pros and cons of simple or complex ideas? Do we even have the disposition to do so? Politicians often claim that if they are in office and something good happens then they should receive credit for it. Many times there is no such connection. Unfortunately, we often fall for such an illusion of causation.

Consumers need to evaluate the claims encountered in the media, in stores, and from other consumers about the efficacy of products and services. Frequently marketers and the media distort the benefits or drawbacks of a product. Can we critically evaluate the claims and the evidence used to support them? When we are told that a study has found that those in Italy who drink more red wine are less likely to have heart disease than those who drink less, do we conclude we should be drinking more red wine? That is not a correct interpretation of the results, but it is easy and tempting to draw such a conclusion.

Again, I am not arguing that acquiring conceptual and procedural knowledge in school is trivial. Rather, the research mentioned previously suggests that acquiring these critical skills are at least as important if not more so than accumulating vast stores of knowledge. Yet, educators devote far more attention to the acquisition of knowledge than to developing skills that are constantly required in virtually every facet of our lives. We need to rethink that.

We need to give these critical skills a proportionate seat at the table. That is, we need to give them at least as much attention in our standards as we do the content of the disciplines. Most state standards bury a limited number of the skills in their content standards. The few skills included tend to be isolated in specific disciplinary areas. For example, my state of Illinois, as articulated by its standards, expects students to "summarize and make generalizations from content and relate them to the purpose of the material," but only in the language arts. Students are also expected to "work cooperatively with others to achieve group goals," but only in the realm of physical education and health. Just because certain skills are not delineated in the state standards does not mean it is not worth teaching them. A librarian or teacher or school can choose to target one or more of these skills to complement the content standards of their district or state.

Although many educators recognize the value of such skills, teachers, library media specialists, and other educators have not been adequately trained in delivering instruction of them. Many do not know how to get started, much less how to integrate skill development systematically into their instruction. Not surprisingly, we return to what is familiar to us; we teach what and how we were taught. That often means using textbook and lecture to impart wagons full of concepts and facts, and giving insufficient attention to critical skill development. Some educators attempt to teach some of these skills, but rarely is such instruction applied systematically and thoroughly. Good skill development requires a great deal of modeling, practice, feedback, and reflection. That takes time, but across 12 years of schooling that time can be found.

THE ROLE OF ASSESSMENT
IN DEVELOPING CRITICAL SKILLS

As educators progress from developing standards to constructing assessments to address the standards, they often ask, "Do we really need to assess that?" If it was important enough to be written into a standard, then, yes, you should want to know if your students are capable of demonstrating competence for that standard. Can they use technology to solve problems or answer questions? Can they evaluate their own work? If you believe such skills are critical for your students' future, you will want to determine if they have acquired these skills.

These skills will not receive the consideration they are due *unless* they are assessed. As we have all seen, those concepts and skills that receive the most attention are the ones that are measured. Moreover, instruction cannot be adjusted and student strategies cannot be adapted without specific feedback offered by the results of regular assessment of these skills. When specific goals are set and regular progress towards those goals is measured greater progress will be found (Locke & Latham, 2002).

Furthermore, as authentic assessment advocates recommend, good curricular and instructional development begins at the end: First, identify where you want students to end up, i.e., what they should know and be able to do in school, work, and life; design assessments that will capture real-world application of that knowledge and skills; and then develop and teach a curriculum that guides students towards authentic demonstration of the skills on the assessment tasks (e.g., Herman, Aschbacher, & Winters, 1992; Wiggins, 1998). So, not only will assessment of these skills ensure more attention to their instruction, but the assessments themselves can serve to effectively guide that instruction and learning.

Unfortunately, many educators are even less familiar with how to assess or evaluate skills such as information literacy, problem-solving, or meta-cognitive strategies than they are at teaching them. So, if they do not know how to assess it, and cannot easily articulate what good performance on such a skill would look like, it is easier for teachers and librarians to avoid it. Teachers often are reluctant to devote class time to a topic if it is not going to be tested and contribute to a grade. Consequently, teachers are less likely to provide sufficient feedback and meaningful opportunities for reflection on skill development.

In other words, assessment is a necessary and critical piece in the development of these skills. Does that require another NCLB-like blast of tests? No, locally created assessments embedded in classroom instruction will provide the best tools for promoting effective teaching and learning of the skills (Popham, 2005). What might such assessment of skill development look like? Since skills involve performance, assessment of skills should be performance oriented. If you want to know if those skills can be competently applied beyond your classroom, you should give students the opportunity to perform them in authentic, real-world contexts. That is the intent of authentic (performance-based) assessment.

Thus, in the remaining chapters I will provide the background assessment knowledge as well as a step-by-step process for creating meaningful assessments of the critical skills. In Chapters 4 and 5, I will lay the foundation for the assessment of critical skills by describing the nature and types of *authentic assessments* and how to create them. In Chapter 6, I will describe how authentic assessments can be applied specifically to skill development. Then, in Chapters 7 through 9, I will target three of the specific skills to provide practical examples of how to design authentic assessments of such skills across the grade levels (K-16).

One point the standards movement has driven home is that we need to have a clear picture of where we want to end up if we want to have a chance of getting there. The target should be clear, significant, and relevant. A corollary to that principle is that it does no good to head down a path towards a goal if we have no way of telling if we have veered off the path, or reached our target. We need to regularly gather information about our progress and any discrepancies between our performance and our goals. In other words, as I will describe in Chapter 6, we need good summative *and* formative assessments all along the way, and I will describe how we can develop and use them.

Additionally, well-designed assessments do more than provide a means of measuring progress. They also:

- Develop student learning
- Provide a clear target
- Provide concrete evidence
- Provide feedback and the opportunity for reflection

I will illustrate how in the following chapters.

Authentic Assessment: What Is It?

4

> *Note: Chapters 4 and 5 are intended to serve as a fairly detailed exposition of authentic assessment to lay the foundation for the subsequent chapters which describe specifically how to authentically assess the critical skills. If you feel sufficiently comfortable with authentic assessments, formative and summative assessments, criteria and rubrics, and the rest, feel free to skip ahead. However, if you find yourself stumbling a bit on the terminology or the process of assessment described in the following chapters, you are always welcome back here for a thorough exploration or a brief refresher. As is common with authentic assessment, I will let you choose your path to constructing knowledge and skills. One other note: Most of this chapter is adapted from my online text, Authentic Assessment Toolbox, which can be found at <http://jonathan.mueller.faculty. noctrl.edu/toolbox>, where you can find an even more thorough explanation of authentic assessment.*

WHAT IS AUTHENTIC ASSESSMENT?

Consider, first, a more common alternative to authentic assessment: Selected-response tests, or what I am calling *traditional assessment*. Test formats such as multiple-choice, T-F or matching require students to select an alternative from two or more choices. As some of you may remember, such tests have also been labeled forced-choice because the test takers are forced to choose from two or more alternatives, as opposed to constructing their own answer in response to a prompt.

A traditional test is an efficient means of discovering whether students have acquired a certain body of knowledge. With carefully crafted questions, traditional assessment can also provide some limited evidence of higher-level thinking about a concept, a principle, or a process (Haladyna, 1999).

However, the primary type of evidence we are asked to provide in everyday life is rarely a selected response. Instead, we are asked to use knowledge and skill to perform a variety of tasks. We are continually asked to apply what we have learned, which is the essence of authentic assessment. Specifically,

> *Authentic assessment is a form of assessment in which students are asked to perform real-world tasks that demonstrate meaningful application of essential knowledge and skills.*

For example, instead of selecting the correct answer on a test of computing percentages (traditional assessment), a student might be asked to justify the purchase of several pieces of clothing at one store versus another given the respective sales (% off) at the two stores (authentic assessment). Or, instead of recognizing the names and significant events of a particular period of American history, a student might be asked to construct a newspaper article from a certain era reflecting their grasp of the issues and events of the period.

TYPES OF AUTHENTIC ASSESSMENTS

Authentic assessments can be employed to measure performance on virtually any behavior in which we engage. That means students (or employees) can be asked to complete tasks ranging from brief ones such as paraphrasing an argument to more elaborate products or performances requiring the complex integration of knowledge and skills. This range of tasks is described in the following sections within three common categories of authentic assessments along with common examples of each.

CONSTRUCTED RESPONSE

In response to a prompt, students construct an answer out of old and new knowledge. Since there is no one exact answer to these prompts, students are constructing new knowledge that likely differs slightly or significantly from that constructed by other students. Typically, constructed response prompts are narrowly conceived, delivered at or near the same time a response is expected, and are limited in length. However, the fact that students must construct new knowledge means that at least some of their thinking must be revealed. As opposed to selected response items, the teacher gets to look inside the students' heads a little with constructed response answers to identify processes utilized and misconceptions harbored.

Examples include:

(Product-Like)
- Short-answer essay questions
- "Show your work"
- Concept maps
- Figural representation (e.g., Venn diagram)
- Journal response

(Performance-Like)

- Typing test
- Complete a step of science lab
- On demand, construct a short musical, dance or dramatic response
- On demand, exhibit an athletic skill

Constructed response items simulate many everyday tasks which involve a brief demonstration of a skill or application of knowledge such as deciding between two choices, or interpreting a political cartoon, or finding a relationship between two or more ideas. For example, to replicate a scientific thinking task we encounter quite often in our daily lives, I present my students with a claim made in the media and ask them to determine if the evidence given to support the claim is appropriate and sufficient.

PRODUCT

In response to a prompt (assignment) or series of prompts, students construct a substantial, tangible product that reveals their understanding of certain concepts and skills and their ability to apply, analyze, synthesize, or evaluate those concepts and skills. It is similar to a constructed-response item in that students are required to construct new knowledge and not just select a response. However, product assessments typically are more substantial in depth and length, more broadly conceived, and allow more time between the presentation of the prompt and the student response than constructed-response items.

Examples include:

- Essays, stories or poems
- Research reports
- Extended journal responses
- Art exhibit or portfolio
- Lab reports
- Newspaper
- Poster

In the workplace, we are often required to research a topic and produce a report or present the findings; find solutions to problems; and evaluate the ideas and work of others. Asking students to create such products prepares them for future work and school and permits us to assess their current competence on those authentic tasks.

PERFORMANCE

In response to a prompt (assignment) or series of prompts, students construct a performance that reveals their understanding of certain concepts and skills and their ability to apply, analyze, synthesize, or evaluate those concepts and skills. It is similar to a constructed-response item in that students are required to construct new knowledge and not just select a response. However, performances typically are more substantial in depth and length, more broadly conceived, and allow more time between the presentation of the prompt and the student response than constructed-response items.

Examples include:

- Conducting an experiment
- Musical, dance, or dramatic performances
- Debates
- Athletic competition
- Oral presentation

Consider how often we are called upon to build or fix something, to carry out a process or follow the steps of a procedure, to express ourselves individually or collectively through a variety of media. Preparing students for such future performances is preparing them for the real world. Assessing students on critical performances provides the opportunity to give them meaningful feedback to further develop these skills.

All of these types of authentic tasks capture real-world application of knowledge and skills as opposed to the less authentic selection of a correct response on a test.

CHARACTERISTICS OF AUTHENTIC ASSESSMENT

Another way that authentic assessment is commonly distinguished from traditional assessment is in terms of their defining attributes. Of course, traditional assessments as well as authentic assessments vary considerably in the forms they take. Yet, typically, along the continuums of attributes listed below, traditional assessments fall more towards the left end of each continuum and authentic assessments fall more towards the right end.

Traditional		Authentic
Selecting a Response	- - - - - - - - - - - - - - -	Performing a Task
Contrived	- - - - - - - - - - - - - - -	Real-Life
Recall/Recognition	- - - - - - - - - - - - - - -	Construction/Application
Teacher-Structured	- - - - - - - - - - - - - - -	Student-Structured
Indirect Evidence	- - - - - - - - - - - - - - -	Direct Evidence

Let me clarify the attributes by elaborating on each in the context of traditional and authentic assessments:

Selecting a Response to Performing a Task: On traditional assessments, students are typically given several choices (e.g., a, b, c or d; true or false;

which of these match with those) and asked to select the right answer. In contrast, authentic assessments ask students to demonstrate understanding by performing a more complex task usually representative of more meaningful application.

Contrived to Real-Life: It is not very often in life outside of school that we are asked to select from four alternatives to indicate our proficiency at something. Tests offer these contrived means of assessment to increase the number of times you can be asked to demonstrate proficiency in a short period of time. More commonly in life, as in authentic assessments, we are asked to demonstrate proficiency by doing something.

Recall/Recognition of Knowledge to Construction/Application of Knowledge: Well-designed traditional assessments (i.e., tests and quizzes) can effectively determine whether or not students have acquired a body of knowledge. Thus, tests can serve as a nice complement to authentic assessments in a teacher's assessment portfolio. Furthermore, we *are* often asked to recall or recognize facts and ideas and propositions in life, so tests are somewhat authentic in that sense. However, the demonstration of recall and recognition on tests is typically much less revealing about what we really know and can do than when we are asked to construct a product or performance out of facts, ideas, and propositions. Authentic assessments often ask students to analyze, synthesize, and apply what they have learned in a substantial manner, and students create new meaning in the process as well.

Teacher-Structured to Student-Structured: When completing a traditional assessment, what a student can and will demonstrate has been carefully structured by the person(s) who developed the test. A student's attention will understandably be focused on and limited to what is on the test. In contrast, authentic assessments allow more student choice and construction in determining what is presented as evidence of proficiency. Even when students cannot choose their own topics or formats, there are usually multiple acceptable routes towards constructing a product or performance. Obviously, assessments more carefully controlled by the teachers offer advantages and disadvantages. Similarly, more student-structured tasks have strengths and weaknesses that must be considered when choosing and designing an assessment.

Indirect Evidence to Direct Evidence: Even if a multiple-choice question asks a student to analyze or apply facts to a new situation rather than just recall the facts, and the student selects the correct answer, what do you now know about that student? Did that student get lucky and pick the right answer? What thinking led the student to pick that answer? We really do not know. At best, we can make some inferences about what that student might know and might be able to do with that knowledge. The evidence is very indirect, particularly for claims of meaningful application in complex, real-world situations. Authentic assessments, on the other hand, offer more direct evidence of application and construction of knowledge. For example, putting a golf student on the golf course to play provides much more direct evidence of proficiency than giving the student a written test. Can a student effectively critique the arguments someone else has presented (an important skill often required in the real world)? Asking a student to write a critique should provide more direct evidence of that skill than asking the student a series of multiple-choice, analytical questions about a passage, although both assessments may be useful.

TEACHING TO THE TEST

These two different approaches to assessment also offer different advice about teaching to the test. Under the traditional assessment model, teachers have been discouraged from teaching to the test. That is because a test usually assesses a sample of students' knowledge and understanding and assumes that students' performance on the sample is representative of their knowledge of all the relevant material. If teachers focus primarily on the sample to be tested during instruction, then good performance on that sample does not necessarily reflect knowledge of all the material. So, teachers hide the test so that the sample is not known beforehand, and teachers are admonished not to teach to the test.

With authentic assessment, teachers are *encouraged* to teach to the test. Students need to learn how to perform well on meaningful tasks. To aid students in that process, it is helpful to show them models of good (and not so good) performance. Furthermore, the student benefits from seeing the task rubric ahead of time as well. Is this "cheating"? Will students then just be able to mimic the work of others without truly understanding what they are doing? Authentic assessments typically do not lend themselves to mimicry. There is no one correct answer to copy. So, by knowing what good performance looks like, and by knowing what specific characteristics make up good performance, students can better develop the skills and understanding necessary to perform well on these tasks.

AUTHENTIC ASSESSMENT
COMPLEMENTS TRADITIONAL ASSESSMENT

Although I have contrasted authentic and traditional assessment along several dimensions and positioned them as serving competing philosophies, this is ultimately a false dichotomy; the choice is not between using traditional or authentic assessment. Educators have learned that one form of assessment can complement or supplement the other. For example, the following questions on a selected-response test of information literacy can inform you about whether students possess some necessary vocabulary (e.g., what's a periodical?) to navigate the process of finding useful information.

Which of the following is a periodical?

   a. *Newsweek Magazine*

   b. The fifth edition of *MLA Handbook*

   c. *The Statesman's Yearbook*

   d. *Periodical Abstracts*

I would be most likely to find a good overview article on my topic along with a bibliography of additional resources in

   a. a Web site

   b. a reference book

   c. a magazine

   d. a scholarly journal

Which type of search will retrieve the most relevant items to your topic?

   a. Keyword

   b. Subject

   c. Title Words

   d. Author

Questions courtesy of North Central College Library Services

To complement such a traditional test of information literacy knowledge, students can additionally be authentically assessed on their ability to frame a question, identify appropriate sources of information, locate and access information from those sources, and evaluate the accuracy, authority, relevancy, and currency of the information as it pertains to the original question.

SUMMATIVE AND FORMATIVE ASSESSMENTS

An authentic assessment or a traditional assessment or some combination of the two can be used to determine if students have satisfactorily met certain standards at the end of some period of time (e.g., unit, semester, year, graduation). Such a cumulative assessment is commonly called a *summative* assessment because it provides a summary judgment of the students' final competencies; it is an assessment *of* learning.

Of course, if you wait until the end of a time period to determine if students are meeting the standards, there will be no time for the teacher to adjust instruction or the student to adjust strategies to address any deficiencies. Consequently, it is highly recommended that *formative* assessments, or checks for understanding, be administered regularly throughout the time period to inform teacher and student of progress made, deficiencies found, and the need for new approaches or additional instruction or practice (Black & Wiliam, 1998; Chappuis & Chappuis, 2007/2008; Marzano, 2006); thus, they are assessments *for* learning. Formative assessments are typically embedded within instruction so that teaching, checks for understanding, and feedback comprise a single, fluid process of learning rather than serve as standalone events.

How are such authentic assessments, summative or formative, created? A thorough description of that process is presented in the following chapter. Then, a more detailed use of summative and formative assessment will be examined in Chapter 6 in the discussion of how to assess skill development.

Authentic Assessment: How Do You Do It?

5

How Are Authentic Assessments Created?

As described in the *Authentic Assessment Toolbox* (found at <http://jonathan. mueller.faculty.noctrl.edu/toolbox>), I recommend a four-step process for creating an authentic assessment. I tend to think of the four steps in terms of four questions to be asked. Those questions are captured in Figure 5.1.

Figure 5.1: Steps for Creating an Authentic Assessment

QUESTIONS TO ASK:

1) What should students know and be able to do?
This list of knowledge and skills becomes your . . .

STANDARDS

2) What indicates students have met these standards?
To determine if students have met these standards, you will design or select relevant . . .

AUTHENTIC TASKS

3) What does good performance on this task look like?
To determine if students have performed well on the task, you will identify and look for characteristics of good performance called . . .

CRITERIA

4) How well did the students perform?
To discriminate among student performance across criteria, you will create a . . .

RUBRIC

STEP 1: IDENTIFY THE STANDARDS

This step could be as simple as adopting the standards for your discipline or grade or school that were created at the state or national level. However, I find that the most useful standards are the ones developed locally. Standards written a little more narrowly to fit a course or even a unit often provide better guidance for the development of instruction and assessment because they more directly capture what is valued and emphasized in a classroom. Although you may be obligated to adopt and work towards an already accepted set of standards, nothing prevents you from additionally articulating one or more standards for critical skills that you believe are worth pursuing. If you are a library media specialist and your school, district, or state has no explicit standard for information literacy, does that mean you will not collaborate with others to develop those skills?

To generate or adapt your own standards, I recommend a three-step process for writing standards:

1. REFLECT
2. REVIEW
3. WRITE

Reflect

There are many sources you can visit to find examples of goals and standards that might be appropriate for your students. There are national and state standards as well as numerous Web sites with many good choices. It is unnecessary to start from scratch. However, before you look at the work of others, which can confine your thinking, take some time to examine (or *reflect* upon) what *you* value as an educator or school or district. What do you really want your students to know and be able to do when they leave your grade or school?

Here is a sample of questions you might ask yourself:

- What do you want students to come away with from an education at _____ ?
- What should *citizens* know and be able to do?
- If you are writing standards for a particular discipline, what should *citizens* know and be able to do relevant to your discipline?
- What goals and standards do you share with other disciplines?
- What college preparation should you provide?
- Think of a graduate or current student that particularly exemplifies the set of knowledge and skills that will make/has made that student successful in the real world. What knowledge and skills (related and unrelated to your discipline) does that person possess?
- Ask yourself, "above all else, we want to graduate students who can/will _____ ?"

- When you find yourself complaining about what students cannot or do not do, what do you most often identify?

As a result of this reflection, you might reach consensus on a few things you most value and agree should be included in the standards. You might actually write a few standards. Or, you might produce a long list of possible candidates for standards. There is not a particular product you need to generate as a result of the reflection phase. Rather, you should move on to Step 2 (Review) when you are clear about what is most important for your students to learn.

Review

Did you wake up this morning thinking, "Hey, I'm going to reinvent the wheel today?" No need. There are many, many good models of learning goals and standards available to you. So, before you start putting your standards down on paper, *review* what others have developed. For example, you can:

Look at:
- your state goals and standards
- relevant national goals and standards
- other state and local standards already created (e.g., visit <http://edstandards.org/Standards.html>)
- your existing goals and standards, if you have any
- other sources that may be relevant (e.g., what employers want, what colleges want)

Look for:
- descriptions and language that capture what you said you value in Step 1 (Reflect)
- knowledge and skills not captured in the first step—should they be included?
- ways to organize and connect the important knowledge and skills

Look to:
- develop a good sense of the whole picture of what you want your students to know and to do
- identify for which checkpoints (grades) you want to write standards

Write

In standards writing schools and districts often miss the forest for the trees. As with many tasks, too often we get bogged down in the details and lose track of the big picture. It cannot be emphasized enough how important it is to periodically step back and reflect upon the process. As you write your standards, ask yourself and your colleagues *guiding questions* such as:

- So, tell me again, why do we think this is important?
- Realistically, are they ever going to have to know this/do this/use this?
- How does this knowledge/skill relate to this standard over here?
- We don't have a standard about X; is this really more important than X?
- Can we really assess this? Should we assess it?
- Is this knowledge or skill essential for becoming a productive citizen? How? Why?
- Is this knowledge or skill essential for college preparation?

Yes, you may annoy your colleagues with these questions (particularly if you ask them repeatedly as I would advocate), but you will end up with a better set of standards that will last longer and provide a stronger foundation for the steps that follow in the creation of performance assessments.

For more details on writing good standards, see the *Authentic Assessment Toolbox* at <http://jonathan.mueller.faculty.noctrl.edu/toolbox>.

STEP 2: SELECTING AN AUTHENTIC TASK

If you completed Step 1 (identify the standards) successfully, then the remaining three steps, particularly this one, will be much easier. With each step it is helpful to return to your goals and standards for direction. For example, imagine that one of your standards is:

> *Students will describe the geographic, economic, social, and political consequences of the Revolutionary War.*

In Step 2, you want to find a way students can demonstrate that they are fully capable of meeting the standard. The language of a well-written standard can spell out what a task should ask students to do to demonstrate their mastery of it. For the above standard it is as simple as saying the task should ask students to *describe the geographic, economic, social, and political consequences of the Revolutionary War*. That might take the form of an analytic paper you assign, a multimedia presentation students develop (individually or collaboratively), a debate they participate in, or even an essay question on a test.

Starting from Scratch? Look at Your Standards

What if you do not currently have an authentic assessment for a particular standard? How do you create one from scratch? Again, start with your standard. What does it ask your students to do?

A good authentic task would ask them to demonstrate what the standard expects of students.

For example, the standard might state that students will:

solve problems involving fractions using addition, subtraction, multiplication, and division.

Teachers commonly ask students to do just that—solve problems involving fractions. That is an authentic task.

Starting from Scratch? Look at the Real World

But what if you want a more engaging task for your students? A second method of developing an authentic task from scratch is by asking the question "Where would they use these skills in the real world?" For computing with fractions teachers have asked students to follow recipes, order or prepare pizzas, and measure and plan the painting or carpeting of a room. Each of these tasks is not just an instructional activity; each can also be an authentic assessment.

STEP 3: IDENTIFYING THE CRITERIA FOR THE TASK

In Step 1, you identified what you want your students to know and be able to do. In Step 2, you selected a task (or tasks) students would perform or produce to demonstrate that they have met the standard from Step 1. For Step 3, you want to ask "What does good performance on this task look like?" or "How will I know they have done a good job on this task?" In answering those questions you will be identifying the *criteria* for good performance on that task. You will use those criteria to evaluate how well students completed the task and, thus, how well they have met the standard or standards.

Examples

Example 1

Here is a *standard* from a high school special education curriculum:

> *The student will conduct banking transactions.*

The *authentic task* this teacher assigned to students to assess the standard was to make deposits, withdrawals, or cash checks at a bank.

To identify the *criteria* for good performance on this task, the teacher asked herself "What would good performance on this task look like?" She came up with seven essential characteristics for successful completion of the task:

- Selects needed form (deposit, withdrawal)
- Fills in form with necessary information
- Endorses check
- Locates open teller
- States type of transaction

- Counts money to be deposited to teller
- Puts money received in wallet

If students meet these criteria then they have performed well on the task and, thus, have met the standard or, at least, provided some evidence of meeting the standard.

Example 2

Here are six standards from a geometry course. Students will be able to:

- *measure quantities using appropriate units, instruments, and methods*
- *set up and solve proportions*
- *develop scale models*
- *estimate amounts and determine levels of accuracy needed*
- *organize materials*
- *explain their thought process*

The *authentic task* used to assess these standards in a geometry class was the following:

Rearrange the Room

You want to rearrange the furniture in some room in your house, but your parents do not think it would be a good idea. To help persuade your parents to rearrange the furniture you are going to make a two-dimensional scale model of what the room would ultimately look like.

Procedure:

1) *You first need to measure the dimensions of the floor space in the room you want to rearrange, including the location and dimensions of all doors and windows. You also need to measure the amount of floor space occupied by each item of furniture in the room. These dimensions should all be explicitly listed.*

2) *Then use the given proportion to find the scale dimensions of the room and all the items.*

3) *Next you will make a scale blueprint of the room labeling where all windows and doors are on poster paper.*

4) *You will also make scale drawings of each piece of furniture on a cardboard sheet of paper, and cut out the models.*

5) *Then you will arrange the model furniture where you want it on your blueprint, and tape them down.*

6) *You will finally write a brief explanation of why you believe the furniture should be arranged the way it is in your model.*

Your models and explanations will be posted in the room and the class will vote on which setup is the best.

Finally, the *criteria* that the teacher identified as indicators of good performance on the *Rearrange the Room* task were:

- accuracy of calculations
- accuracy of measurements on the scale model
- labels on the scale model
- organization of calculations
- neatness of drawings
- clear explanations

You may have noticed in the second example that some of the standards and some of the criteria sounded quite similar. For example, one standard said students will be able to *develop scale models*, and two of the criteria were *accuracy of measurements on the scale model* and *labels on the scale model*. Is this redundant? No, it means that your criteria are aligned with your standards. You are actually measuring on the task what you said you valued in your standards.

Characteristics of a Good Criterion

So, what does a good criterion (singular of criteria) look like? It should be:

- clearly stated
- brief
- observable
- a statement of behavior
- written in language students understand

Additionally, make sure each criterion is distinct. Although the criteria for a single task will understandably be related to one another, there should not be too much overlap between them. Are you really looking for different aspects of performance on the task with the different criteria, or does one criterion simply rephrase another one? For example, the following criteria might be describing the same behavior depending on what you are looking for:

- interpret the data
- draw a conclusion from the data

Another overlap occurs when one criterion is actually a subset of another criterion.

For example, the first criterion below probably subsumes the second:

- presenter keeps the audience's attention
- presenter makes eye contact with the audience

Like standards, criteria should be shared with students *before* they begin a task so they know the teacher's expectations and have a clearer sense of what good performance should look like. Some teachers go further and involve the students in identifying appropriate criteria for a task. The teacher might ask the students "What characteristics does a good paper have?" or "What should I see in a good scale model?" or "How will I (or anyone) know you have done a good job on this task?"

How Many Criteria Do You Need for a Task?

There is not an easy answer to that question, but here are some guidelines:

- **Limit the number of criteria; keep it to the essential elements of the task.** This is a guideline, not a rule. On a major, complex task you might choose 50 different attributes you are looking for in a good performance. That is fine. Generally, assessment will be more feasible and meaningful if you focus on the important characteristics of the task. Typically, you will have fewer than 10 criteria for a task, and many times it might be as few as three or four.
- **You do not have to assess everything on every task.** For example, you might value correct grammar and spelling in all writing assignments, but you do not have to look for those criteria in every assignment. You have made it clear to your students that you expect good grammar and spelling in every piece of writing, but you only check for it in some of them. That way, you are assessing those characteristics in the students' writing and you are sending the message that you value those elements, but you do not take the time of grading them on every assignment.
- **Smaller, less significant tasks typically require fewer criteria.** For short homework or in-class assignments you might only need a quick check on the students' work. Two or three criteria might be sufficient to judge the understanding or application you were after in that task. Less significant tasks require less precision in your assessment than larger, more comprehensive tasks that are designed to assess significant progress toward multiple standards.

Have I Created a Good Set of Criteria for the Task?

Ask yourself. You have to apply the criteria. Do they make sense to you? Can you distinguish one from another? Can you envision examples of each? Are they all worth assessing?

Ask your students. Do they make sense to them? Do they understand their relationship to the task? Do they know how they would use the criteria to begin their work? Do they know how they would use the criteria to check their work?

Ask your colleagues. Ask those who give similar assignments. Ask others who are unfamiliar with the subject matter to get a different perspective if you like.

If you have assigned a certain task before, go back and review previous student work. Do these criteria capture the elements of what you considered good work? Are you missing anything essential?

STEP 4: CREATING A RUBRIC

In Step 1 of creating an authentic assessment, you identified what you wanted your students to know and be able to do—your standards.

In Step 2, you asked how students could demonstrate that they had met your standards. As a result, you developed authentic tasks they could perform.

In Step 3, you identified the characteristics of good performance on the authentic task—the criteria.

Now, in Step 4, you will finish creating the authentic assessment by constructing a rubric to measure student performance on the task. To build the rubric, you will begin with the set of criteria you identified in Step 3. As mentioned before, keep the number of criteria manageable. You do not have to look for everything on every assessment.

Once you have identified the criteria you want to look for as indicators of good performance, you next decide whether to consider the criteria analytically or holistically.

Creating an Analytic Rubric

In an analytic rubric, performance is judged separately for each criterion. Teachers assess how well students meet a criterion on a task, distinguishing between work that effectively meets the criterion, and work that does not meet it. The next step in creating a rubric, then, is deciding how fine such a distinction should be made for each criterion. For example, if you are judging the amount of eye contact a presenter made with his audience, that judgment could be as simple as did or did not make eye contact (two levels of performance), never, sometimes, or always made eye contact (three levels), or never, rarely, sometimes, usually, or always made eye contact (five levels).

Generally, it is better to start small with fewer levels because it is usually harder to make finer distinctions. For eye contact, I might begin with three levels such as never, sometimes, and usually. Then if, in applying the rubric, I found that some students seemed to fall in between never and sometimes, and never or sometimes did not adequately describe the students' performance, I could add a fourth (e.g., rarely) and, possibly, a fifth level to the rubric.

In other words, there is some trial and error that must go on to arrive at the most appropriate number of levels for a criterion.

Do I Need to Have the Same Number of Levels of Performance for Each Criterion within a Rubric?

No. You could have five levels of performance for three criteria in a rubric, three levels for two other criteria, and four levels for another criterion, all within the same rubric. Rubrics are very flexible tools. There is no need to force an unnatural judgment of performance just to maintain standardization within the rubric. If one criterion is a simple either/or judgment and another criterion requires finer distinctions, then the rubric can reflect that variation.

Do I Need to Add Descriptors to Each Level of Performance?

No. Descriptors are recommended but not required in a rubric. Descriptors are the characteristics of behavior associated with specific levels of performance for specific criteria. For example, in the elementary science rubric illustrated in Figure 5.2, the criteria are 1) made good observations 2) made good predictions, and 3) appropriate conclusions. Labels (limited, acceptable, proficient) for the different levels of performance are also included. Under each label, for each criterion, a descriptor is included to further explain what performance *at that level* looks like.

Figure 5.2: Rubric with Descriptors

Criteria	Limited	Acceptable	Proficient
made good observations	observations are absent or vague	most observations are clear and detailed	all observations are clear and detailed
made good predictions	predictions are absent or irrelevant	most predictions are reasonable	all predictions are reasonable
appropriate conclusion	conclusion is absent or inconsistent with observations	conclusion is consistent with most observations	conclusion is consistent with observations

As you can imagine, students will be more certain what is expected to reach each level of performance on the rubric if descriptors are provided. Furthermore, the more detail a teacher provides about what good performance looks like on a task the better a student can approach the task. Teachers benefit as well when descriptors are included. A teacher is likely to be more objective and consistent when applying a descriptor such as "most observations are clear and detailed" than when applying a simple label such as "acceptable." Similarly, if more than one teacher is using the same rubric, the specificity of the descriptors increases the chances that multiple teachers will apply the rubric in a similar manner. When a rubric is applied more consistently and objectively, it will lead to greater reliability and validity in the results.

Assigning Point Values to Performance on Each Criterion

Rubrics are very flexible tools. Just as the number of levels of performance can vary from criterion to criterion in an analytic rubric, points or value can be assigned to the rubric in myriad ways. For example, a teacher who creates a rubric might decide that certain criteria are more important to the overall performance on the task than other criteria. So, one or more criteria can be weighted more heavily when scoring the performance. For example, in a rubric for solo auditions, a teacher might consider five criteria: (how well students demonstrate) vocal tone, vocal technique, rhythm, diction, and musicality. For this teacher, musicality might be the most important quality that she has stressed and is looking for in the audition. She might consider vocal technique to be less important than musicality but more important than the other criteria. So, she might give musicality and vocal technique more weight in her rubric. She can assign weights in different ways. Figure 5.3 illustrates one common format.

Figure 5.3: Rubric 1 for Solo Audition

Solo Audition							
	0	1	2	3	4	5	weight
vocal tone							
vocal technique								x2
rhythm							
diction							
musicality								x3

In this case, placement in the 4-point level for vocal tone would earn the student four points for that criterion. But placement in the 4-point box for vocal technique would earn the student eight points, and placement in the 4-point box for musicality would earn the student 12 points. The same weighting could also be displayed as follows in Figure 5.4.

Figure 5.4: Rubric 2 for Solo Audition

Solo Audition					
	NA	Poor	Fair	Good	Very Good	Excellent
vocal tone	0	1	2	3	4	5
vocal technique	0	2	4	6	8	10
rhythm	0	1	2	3	4	5
diction	0	1	2	3	4	5
musicality	0	3	6	9	12	15

In both examples, musicality is worth three times as many points as vocal tone, rhythm and diction, and vocal technique is worth twice as much as each of those criteria. Pick a format that works for you and your students. There is no "correct" format in the layout of rubrics. So, choose one or design one that meets your needs.

Yes, But Do I Need Equal Intervals Between the Point Values in a Rubric?
No. Say it with me one more time—rubrics are flexible tools. Shape them to fit your needs, not the other way around. In other words, points should be distributed across the levels of a rubric to best capture the value you assign to each level of performance. For example, points might be awarded on an oral presentation as follows in Figure 5.5.

Figure 5.5: Rubric for Oral Presentation

Oral Presentation			
Criteria	never	sometimes	always
makes eye contact	0	3	4
volume is appropriate	0	2	4
enthusiasm is evident	0	2	4
summary is accurate	0	4	8

In other words, you might decide that at this point in the year you would be pleased if a presenter makes eye contact "sometimes," so you award that level of performance most of the points available. However, "sometimes" would not be as acceptable for level of volume or enthusiasm.
    Here are some more examples of rubrics illustrating the flexibility of number of levels and value you assign each level.

Figure 5.6: Rubric with Varying Number of Levels of Performance and Weights

Oral Presentation			
Criteria	never	sometimes	usually
makes eye contact	0	2	4
volume is appropriate	0		4
enthusiasm is evident	0		4
summary is accurate	0	4	8

As shown in the Figure 5.6 rubric, you have decided to measure volume and enthusiasm at two levels—never or usually—whereas, you are considering eye contact and accuracy of summary across three levels. That is acceptable if that fits the type of judgments you want to make. Even though there are only two levels for volume and three levels for eye contact, you are awarding the same number of points for a judgment of "usually" for both criteria. However, you could vary that as well, as shown in Figure 5.7.

Figure 5.7: Rubric with Varying Weight per Criterion

Oral Presentation			
Criteria	never	sometimes	usually
makes eye contact	0	2	4
volume is appropriate	0		2
enthusiasm is evident	0		2
summary is accurate	0	4	8

In this case, you have decided to give less weight to volume and enthusiasm as well as to judge those criteria across fewer levels.

So, do not feel bound by any format constraints when constructing a rubric. The rubric should best capture what you value in performance on the authentic task. The more accurately your rubric captures what you want your students to know and be able to do the more valid the scores will be.

Creating a Holistic Rubric

In a holistic rubric, a judgment of how well someone has performed on a task considers all the criteria together, or holistically, instead of separately as in an analytic rubric. Thus, each level of performance in a holistic rubric reflects behavior across all the criteria. For example, here is a holistic version of the oral presentation rubric in Figure 5.7.

Figure 5.8: Holistic Rubric

Oral Presentation Rubric	
Mastery • always makes eye contact • volume is always appropriate • enthusiasm is present throughout presentation • summary is completely accurate	Developing • sometimes makes eye contact • volume is sometimes appropriate • occasional enthusiasm in presentation • some errors in summary
Proficiency • usually makes eye contact • volume is usually appropriate • enthusiasm is present in most of presentation • only one or two errors in summary	Inadequate • never or rarely makes eye contact • volume is inappropriate • rarely shows enthusiasm in presentation • many errors in summary

An obvious, potential problem with applying the rubric in Figure 5.8 is that performance often does not fall neatly into categories such as mastery or proficiency. A student might always make eye contact, use appropriate volume regularly, occasionally show enthusiasm, and include many errors in the summary. Where would you put that student in the holistic rubric? Thus, it is recommended that the use of holistic rubrics be limited to situations when the educator wants to:

- make a quick, holistic judgment that carries little weight in evaluation
- evaluate performance in which the criteria cannot be easily separated

Quick, holistic judgments are often made for homework problems or journal assignments. To allow the judgment to be quick and to reduce the problem illustrated in the above rubric of fitting the best category to the performance, the number of criteria should be limited. For example, Figure 5.9 is a possible holistic rubric for grading homework problems.

Figure 5.9: Holistic Rubric

Homework Problem Rubric		
++ (3 pts.) • most or all answers correct, AND • most or all work shown	+ (1 pt.) • at least some answers correct, AND • at least some but not most work shown	- (0 pts.) • few answers correct, OR • little or no work shown

However, even for a rubric as simple as this homework one, it still is not easy for such a holistic rubric to accurately capture what is valued *and* cover all the possible combinations of student performance. For example, what if a student got all the answers correct on a problem assignment but did not show any work? The rubric covers that: The student would receive a (-) because "little or no work was shown." What if a student showed all the work but only got some of the answers correct? That student would receive a (+) according to the rubric. All such combinations are covered. But does giving a (+) for such work reflect what the teacher values? The rubric in Figure 5.9 is designed to give equal weight to correct answers and work shown. If that is not the teacher's intent, then the rubric needs to be changed to fit the goals of the teacher.

All of this complexity with just two criteria—imagine if a third criterion were added to the rubric. So, with holistic rubrics, limit the number of criteria considered, or consider using an analytic rubric.

Final Step: Checking Your Rubric

As a final check on your rubric, you can do any or all of the following before applying it.

- Let a colleague review it.
- Let your students review it—is it clear to them?
- Check if it aligns or matches up with your standards.
- Check if it is manageable.
- Consider imaginary student performance on the rubric.

Regarding the last suggestion, imagine that a student had met specific levels of performance on each criterion (for an analytic rubric). Then ask yourself if that performance translates into the score that you think is appropriate. For example, on the Oral Presentation Rubric in Figure 5.5, imagine a student scores:

- "sometimes" for eye contact (3 pts.)
- "always" for volume (4 pts.)
- "always" for enthusiasm (4 pts.)
- "sometimes" for summary is accurate (4 pts.)

That student would receive a score of 15 points out of a possible 20 points. Does 75% (15 out of 20) capture that performance for you? Perhaps you think a student should not receive that high of a score with only "sometimes" for the summary. You can adjust for that by increasing the weight you assign that criterion. Or, imagine a student apparently put a lot of work into the homework problems but got few of them correct. Do you think that student should receive some credit? Then you would need to adjust the holistic homework problem rubric shown in Figure 5.9. In other words, it can be very helpful to play out a variety of performance combinations before you actually administer the rubric. It helps you see the forest through the trees.

Of course, you will never know if you really have a good rubric until you apply it. So, do not work to perfect the rubric before you administer it. Get it in good shape and then try it. Find out what needs to be modified and make the appropriate changes.

Rubrics for Younger Students

At all ages, rubrics should be shared with students when a task is first introduced so that students know precisely what is expected of them and what good work on that task entails. That means we need to construct rubrics using language and structure appropriate to the level of the students with which we are working.

Students are never too young for rubrics. Children as young as three or four years of age are capable of understanding and applying simple rating scales. Furthermore, it is never too early to start students thinking about the quality of their performance or behavior. The earlier they begin learning to monitor and evaluate their own performance, the sooner they become less dependent on others to identify weaknesses in their work or behavior, and the quicker they develop strategies for addressing those weaknesses. A rubric is one good tool to help young children learn that process.

However, with less developed language skills, particularly in reading and writing, younger students obviously must be given simple scales that are cognitively and linguistically appropriate. For example, nonverbal scales using smiley faces to represent different levels of performance are often used with young students.

Along with giving your students rubrics they can understand, think about how you can develop *their* use of rubrics. Self-assessment and the application of criteria are also valuable skills that need to be developed. Here are some suggestions for the construction and use of rubrics for and by younger students.

Start with two levels of performance: Young children can understand a checklist. You either completed the work or you did not. You either engaged in appropriate behavior or you did not. You wrote your name on your paper or you did not. A simple checklist requires less language as well. The behavior is listed, and "yes" or "no" columns are checked. Similarly, the use of smiley faces can begin with just a smiley and a frown face before you add a neutral one.

Once students are comfortable with two levels, a third or fourth level can be added if appropriate. However, for younger students, most student work should not require more than three levels of performance.

Review rubric and practice applying it with students: Although students of all ages would benefit from an explanation of a rubric, younger students in particular need to be walked through the purpose, structure, details, and use of a rubric. They should have the rubric in front of them as you describe what it is and model how it will be used.

Furthermore, students will better understand the rubric if they are allowed to apply it themselves. Give them simple samples of work and behavior and let them practice applying the rubrics to the samples. Making it a collaborative activity in which they apply the rubrics in pairs or small groups should further enhance their appreciation and understanding of the rubric as they see and hear their peers apply it as well. Talk with your students about difficulties or confusion they encounter in the process. As a result of this practice, your students will not only better grasp the purpose and meaning of elements of the rubric, they will also learn how to apply the rubric themselves.

Additionally, talk with your students about how they can use the rubric before, during, and after a task. For example, the list of criteria should be a guide in reminding students of what to include as they begin a task, what to consider as they work on the task, and what to go back and check for once they believe they have completed a task. Again, keep the rubric simple so this is feasible for the younger student.

Use first-person language (where appropriate): You should match the language of the rubric to fit the level of your students. For younger students, one way to accomplish this is to switch from the second- or third-person language often found in the criteria and descriptors of rubrics to first-person language. For example, instead of saying "sentences are clearly written," say "I wrote clear sentences." Or, instead of saying "did not listen to partner," say "I did not listen to my partner." Younger students in particular can more easily consider behavior or performance from their own perspective. Additionally, first-person language more directly asks students to reflect on their own performance.

The visual rubrics developed by Suzanne Ratzlaff, Deb Friezen, *and* their students (Ratzlaff & Diercks, 1995) are good examples of rubrics for younger students. Ratzlaff's rubrics for her fourth grade students include "I" statements, are written in language by and for the students, and include graphics that visually describe appropriate work. Examples of these rubrics can also be found online at <http://www.nde.state.ne.us/cba/Goals2000Handbook.pdf > (p. 18-19).

For more details on creating rubrics, see the *Authentic Assessment Toolbox* at <http://jonathan.mueller.faculty.noctrl.edu/toolbox>. Chapter 6 will examine how authentic assessments can be applied to the teaching and assessing of critical skills.

Assessing Skill Development

6

Most educators are familiar with instances of authentic assessment of *content* within the disciplines (e.g., ask elementary science students to present a report describing the diet and feeding habits of an animal of their choosing) or of authentic assessment of *discipline-specific skills* (e.g., ask government students to interpret a political cartoon). In such authentic assessments, students apply the knowledge and skills of the discipline to situations or tasks that replicate real-world challenges. The measurement of skills is particularly well suited to authentic assessment because meaningful demonstration of skill acquisition or development requires a performance of some kind.

Yet, we rarely assess, authentically or otherwise, the critical *cross-curricular skills* described in Chapter 2. Certainly, one reason is the elusive nature of some of these skills that can make it a challenge to find effective measures of assessing them. How would one measure metacognitive abilities or leadership skills or the ability to evaluate the accuracy and relevancy of information? Furthermore, these skills are infrequently included in state goals or standards, so they receive less assessment attention or urgency.

Nevertheless, these critical skills definitely can and should be assessed. To explain how, I will begin by describing the *summative* assessment of skill development, that is, "final" judgments of whether or not a skill has been acquired and can be applied. If, for example, you set a goal of producing students who can assess their own progress and make adjustments when necessary, and you teach those specific skills because you believe they are critical to your students' future success in so many contexts, you will want to know if your students have been successful and met this goal.

Additionally, along the way towards such a goal you will want to check your students' understanding of, and ability to apply, the skill. Thus, I will also address *formative* assessment of skill development, a type of assessment that accompanies instruction and practice. Information gathered through formative assessment *informs* both teacher and student about progress made towards a goal so that teacher instruction and student learning can be adjusted to student needs.

In this chapter I will describe how skills can be assessed summatively and formatively. In the following three chapters I will more specifically illustrate this process through detailed examples of assessment tasks, criteria, and rubrics for the skills of monitoring one's progress and performance (Chapter 7), information literacy (Chapter 8), and collaboration (Chapter 9).

SUMMATIVE ASSESSMENT OF SKILLS

Because skill development so naturally fits with authentic assessment, it makes sense to adapt the four-step process of creating authentic assessments described in Chapter 5 to the summative assessment of skills.

STEP 1: WRITING SKILLS AS STANDARDS

As mentioned in the previous chapter, the process of creating an authentic assessment begins with identifying a good standard (or outcome in higher education), including writing it in observable and measurable language. When assessing content, some educators struggle with writing a standard that captures comprehension of certain material without relying on verbs such as "understand" or "know." They reasonably ask, "What if what I really want is for my students to *understand* a concept or process? How can I state that in an observable form and capture it authentically?"

A simple, direct approach to address that question is to ask "How could the students demonstrate that they understand the concept or process? What would that look like?" For example, if you want students to understand the differences between books, periodicals, and databases, you could ask, "How could they show me they understand the differences between them?" The students could describe the differences between books, periodicals, and databases in a paragraph or two; they could locate each type of resource in a library when asked to; they could identify which type of resource is most likely to contain certain types of information. Each of these statements (i.e., describe the differences between books, periodicals, and databases; locate each type of resource in a library; identify which type of resource is most likely to contain certain types of information) can then serve as a standard to be taught and assessed. They describe observable and measurable behaviors that are important to information literacy.

A similar approach can be followed in writing standards for the critical skills. Do you want students to be reflective learners, good leaders, and information-literate citizens? How could you judge whether or not they are able to do so? Ask, "What do these skills look like if they are done effectively?" "What behaviors are commonly exhibited by reflective learners, good leaders, and information-literate citizens?" That can help you narrow down broad and often nebulous goals such as "being information literate" into more specific and observable standards. For example, in answering these questions, I would argue that an information-literate person should be able to:

- frame a question to be answered
- locate appropriate sources of information
- access information from a variety of sources
- evaluate the accuracy, relevancy, authority, and currency of information
- determine when sufficient information has been acquired to answer the question

Notice, the standards do not say *frame a **reasonable** question to be answered* or ***effectively** locate appropriate sources of information*. Typically, adjectival or adverbial qualifiers such as *good* or *effectively* are not included in standards. The fact that we would want students to perform these tasks *well* is understood. However, you can certainly choose to include such qualifiers if you like.

STEP 2: DESIGNING TASKS TO ASSESS THE SKILLS
In Step 1, an important skill has been identified. How can students demonstrate that they have acquired this skill and apply it in relevant contexts? Give them opportunities to do so. Create simple or complex tasks by asking the questions described in Chapter 5 such as "When would someone ever use this skill?" or "Why would someone ever need to know how to do this?"

Some situations identified by answering such questions will be brief, simple tasks commonly performed. For example, as mentioned earlier, one skill I work to develop in my students is the ability to evaluate claims presented in the media or in the course of an informal conversation. This is a skill they will have many opportunities to apply. Are my students prepared to do so? Are they capable of judging the validity of a claim based upon the evidence presented? To assess this, students can be presented with brief scenarios in political, scientific, or other contexts in which they are asked to evaluate a claim in light of the accompanying evidence. For example, see Figure 6.1 (on page 48).

Figure 6.1: Evaluating a Claim Scenario

A large study in Finland found evidence that people who ate fish less than once a week ran a 31 percent higher chance of mild to severe depression than people who ate it more often.

The researchers concluded that eating fish lowers the risk of depression.

1. Is the researchers' conclusion warranted given the results? Explain.
2. Circle the headline below that you believe BEST fits the research results.
   a. Eating Fish Can Make You Happy
   b. Being Depressed Lowers Fish Consumption
   c. Fish Eaters Are Happier People
3. Explain why you selected that headline.

To serve the function of summatively assessing students, these brief, constructed-response items could be incorporated into a larger test or project so a sufficient number of items could be administered to address the relevant standards. In fact, the item in Figure 6.1 is one of 25 multiple-choice and short-answer essay questions included in a test we give our majors in psychology to assess their scientific thinking.

In other contexts, the skill set needed to address a problem or question may be more extensive and require more time. For example, if someone must support his own claim with evidence, a more complex task, such as a research paper, can be assigned to students to assess whether or not they can apply the full set of information literacy skills in a meaningful context.

Multiple and Varied
To increase the reliability and validity of inferences drawn from student performances on these tasks, the assessments should be multiple and varied (Stiggins, 1987). In fact, using brief constructed-response items (illustrated in Figure 6.1) permits the repeated testing of student skills across a variety of contexts. A single large task enables students to provide evidence they can integrate several skills into a more complex product, but it only provides a single sample of such skill application and integration, limiting the confidence one can have in the reliability and validity of inferences drawn. Along with a research paper, students could also be asked to demonstrate information literacy skills on some smaller research tasks of different types to provide a greater number and variety of pieces of evidence of skill proficiency.

STEP 3: IDENTIFYING THE CRITERIA FOR THE SKILL

Furthermore, just because a student can complete a large task such as a research paper does not in itself indicate proficiency at the complete set of information literacy skills. To determine that, it is necessary to identify the specific characteristics of good performance on that task, that is, the criteria. What are the observable behaviors, the *behavioral indicators,* of proficiency on a particular skill? For example, what does it look like to be proficient at framing a good research question? Criteria of a good research question might include *clarity, a specific focus, appropriate breadth,* and *relevance to the topic.*

Or, what does good collaborative behavior look like? The characteristics of good collaborative behavior, the criteria on which you would judge student performance, might include behaviors such as *involves others in the task, participates without prompting, seriously considers the ideas of others,* and *offers helpful feedback.*

STEP 4: CREATING RUBRICS FOR RATING SKILL PERFORMANCE

Once the criteria for a task have been identified, a rubric, or rating scale, can be used to judge how well someone has met the criteria for performance on that skill task. Authentic assessment of skills does not require a rubric, but the use of rubrics can increase the consistency of application of the criteria (Marzano, 2006). Additionally, by articulating the criteria and the characteristics of good performance at each level (descriptors), those learning and performing the skill and those teaching and assessing it will share a clearly defined picture of what proficiency should look like.

For example, to assess the item in Figure 6.1 on evaluating claims about eating fish and depression, the rubrics in Figures 6.2 and 6.3 were used.

Figure 6.2: Rubric for Evaluation of Research Claims (Question 1)

Rubric for Research Claim Question		
0	**2**	**3**
Answered YES OR Answered NO but provided inadequate explanation	• Answered NO • With adequate support for position	• Answered NO • With excellent support for position

Figure 6.3: Rubric for Evaluation of Research Claims (Questions 2 and 3)

Eating Fish and Depression (Questions 2 and 3)			
0	**1**	**2**	**3**
• Circled incorrect headline	• Circled incorrect headline	• Circled correct headline	• Circled correct headline
• And provided inadequate explanation	• But provided adequate explanation	• And provided adequate explanation	• And provided excellent explanation

To examine how the four steps of creating an authentic assessment of skill development can be implemented, let's look at another example. For Step 1, we will use the information literacy standard: *Students will be able to frame a question to be answered.* To partially assess this standard, we could use the following authentic task (Step 2).

Leon's Research Question

Leon asks you for help. He is assigned to complete a three-to-five page report on something related to the three branches of the U.S. government. Leon tells you that his dad says that judges have too much power and they are running this country. Leon thought the President was supposed to run the country. Shouldn't he be making the decisions? And what does Congress do? Why don't they tell the judges to stop messing things up? So, Leon decided the question he wanted to research was

Question: What could the President do to fix things?

Has Leon identified a good question to guide his research? Why or why not?

Write another question that you think would serve as a good question to guide Leon's research.

To assess student performance on the *Leon's Research Question* task, we will create a simple rubric (Step 4) built on a set of criteria (Step 3) for judging student responses to the task prompt.

Figure 6.4: Rubric for Developing a Research Question

	Beginning	Developing	Proficient
Criteria			
Leon's question:			
Clear focus	Difficult to identify focus of investigation		Easy to identify focus of investigation
Relevant to topic	Not related to intended focus	Somewhat related to intended focus	Question captures intended focus
Appropriate breadth	Far too narrow or broad for assignment	Somewhat too narrow or broad for assignment	Breadth of question consistent with assignment
New question:			
Clear focus	Difficult to identify focus of investigation		Easy to identify focus of investigation
Relevant to topic	Not related to intended focus	Somewhat related to intended focus	Question captures intended focus
Appropriate breadth	Far too narrow or broad for assignment	Somewhat too narrow or broad for assignment	Breadth of question consistent with assignment

With brief constructed-response items like the *Research Question* task, we can determine if students are capable of distinguishing a good question from a poor one. We can also assess students' ability to frame their own questions for a research topic. Thus, we will have collected good, sufficient, evidence to summatively assess the application of this critical skill.

FORMATIVE ASSESSMENT OF SKILLS

Before someone can reach proficiency on a skill, he needs to learn and practice all of the subskills comprising the larger skill and learn how to combine the subskills effectively. Obviously, educators and students do not want to wait for a summative assessment to learn if these earlier steps have been completed successfully. Thus, formative assessment, the checking of progress to inform instruction and learning, needs to be carried out during the learning of the skill (Black & Wiliam, 1998). Educators *and* students need to continuously consider and reconsider where they are headed, where they are now, and what they need to do to close that gap (Chappuis & Chappuis, 2007/2008).

FOUR STEPS OF SKILL DEVELOPMENT

As mentioned in Chapter 4 and illustrated in the previous section, the teaching, learning, and assessment of skills should be integrated into a single, fluid process. In fact, assessment tends to be a more useful tool when it is embedded throughout the teaching and learning process (Black and Wiliam, 1998). Thus, another way to look at the assessment of skill development is to examine how assessment can play a critical role in each of the four steps of skill development: 1) instruction/modeling, 2) practice, 3) feedback, and 4) reflection.

Step 1: Instruction/Modeling

Obviously, the skill to be learned first must be described or explained or illustrated for the student. Instruction or modeling should include clear samples of good performance of the skill, illustration of its application in relevant contexts, and elucidation of any specific steps that are required in the application of the skill. For example, from Willingham's (2007) review of research on teaching critical thinking strategies, he suggests

> A plausible approach to teaching them is to make them explicit, and to proceed in stages. The first time (or several times) the concept is introduced, explain it with at least two different examples (possibly examples based on students' experiences, as discussed above), label it so as to identify it as a strategy that can be applied in various contexts, and show how it applies to the course content at hand. In future instances, try naming the appropriate critical-thinking strategy to see if students remember it and can figure out how it applies to the material under discussion. With still more practice, students may see which strategy applies without a cue from you.

Prior to instruction, it may be useful to administer a pre-test of the skill(s) to a) determine the level of proficiency among the student population with whom you are working so that you can adjust instruction appropriately, and b) measure growth in the skill acquisition from the pre-test to a summative post-test, and to intermediary checks along the way. If the pre-test is for the latter purpose, it should closely match the post-test. A good discussion and example of the use of such a pre- and post-test (Popham, 2005) can be found at <http://tinyurl.com/5co9p>.

Step 2: Practice

As mentioned in Chapter 4, authentic assessment encourages educators to "teach to the test." You likely have in mind or have developed a summative assessment of a skill before you begin teaching it. Students need plenty of practice of the very skills they will be asked to demonstrate on the summative assessment. Thus, give them scenarios or tasks similar to the ones on the final "test."

However, before students are ready to tackle complex tasks they need to learn about and practice the subskills of a larger skill domain. Before you can swing a tennis racket correctly, you need to learn the grip, footwork, and all the rest. Before you can find useful information, you need to learn to determine what is useful, how to locate appropriate sources, and more.

Thus, to teach these skills to students and to formatively assess their progress on them, you need to give them opportunities to play with each of the pieces of the larger task. In other words, lots of brief constructed-response items are ideal. For example, if you want students to learn to evaluate the relevancy of information for answering a certain question, you can give them a series of pieces or sources of information and ask them to evaluate the relevancy of each one against a given question with a simple rating on a scale or in a paragraph; with a partner or alone.

Practice should not just be drill. Students will acquire the skills and their significance more quickly if they think about their use. For example, if you want students to recognize the importance of framing a clear question before seeking information about it, you can ask them to evaluate the relevancy of a piece or source of information *without* giving them the question. Perhaps with some assistance, students should recognize that it is impossible to determine what "useful" information is until they know for what purpose it is to be used.

Practice needs to be frequent and systematic, with each opportunity to practice or observe a model building upon prior learning. Just as in the acquisition of knowledge, the creation of new schemas for skills is a slow and constructive process. Additionally, applying the skills to a *variety* of tasks, including multiple-choice questions focused on relevant scenarios, enhance the students' ability to make sense of and apply the skills. For example, I present my students with the following multiple-choice question, not to summatively assess them but to give them more practice applying scientific thinking skills.

> Researchers hypothesized that teenage children of parents who had a more lenient curfew would be more likely to experiment with illegal drugs. To test the hypothesis, the researchers surveyed 600 parents, asking them, among other questions, what their curfew was for their teenage children. The researchers also surveyed the teenage children of the parents, asking them, among other questions, whether or not they had experimented with illegal drugs. The researchers then compared the responses of the parents with those of their children.
>
> Did the researchers choose a research method consistent with their hypothesis?
>   a. yes, the hypothesis was correlational and the methodology was correlational in nature
>   b. yes, the hypothesis was causal and the methodology was explanatory
>   c. no, the hypothesis was correlational but the research was not designed to address it
>   d. no, the hypothesis was causal but the research was not designed to address it

Step 3: Feedback

Students can be given ample opportunity to practice a skill, but if that practice is not accompanied by meaningful feedback it is much less likely to be successful. In fact, formative assessment has been found to be such a critical element of effective instruction primarily because of the value of good feedback (Black and Wiliam, 1998).

Feedback from and about performance provides teacher and student with critical information to make the adjustments necessary to build upon prior learning. However, it is not the case that any information or feedback is good feedback. Feedback can even have a negative impact on student attitudes and learning (Kluger and DeNisi, 1996). Thus, it is critical to know how best to deliver feedback. Fortunately, a picture is emerging about when feedback can be harmful or helpful.

Focus on the Task, Not the Person

In general, feedback is less helpful, and can even be harmful, if it focuses on the *person* performing the task rather than the task itself. Feedback such as "You are doing well," or "You haven't shown much improvement on this task," or "Your performance is falling behind others in the class" or "You don't seem to be catching on to this" not only provides little information about how to improve, such comments draw attention to the self. As remarkable as the human brain is at processing and storing information, its capacity to consciously attend to tasks at hand is quite limited. Thus, any distractions from the task can severely limit our ability to attend to what we are doing (e.g., Baumeister, Bratslavsky, Muraven, & Tice, 1998; Muraven, Tice, & Baumeister, 1998). Attention to and concern about the self depletes precious resources needed to sustain focus on the task.

Furthermore, Dweck and her colleagues discovered that praise "can be dangerous" if it highlights characteristics of the self that students perceive as inflexible such as ability (e.g., "Good job; you're smart!"). Students receiving such praise were less likely to persist on tasks, less likely to choose challenging tasks in the future, and more likely to cheat. On the other hand, praise that targeted characteristics more closely associated with the task such as effort and strategies enhanced students' desire for harder problems to take home for practice and their subsequent performance (Dweck, 1999).

Similarly, research on feedback and praise finds that the effects of each can be even more debilitating if it is normative in nature. That is, the more we provide feedback that focuses students' attention on how well they are doing relative to others the less effective it is (Black & William, 1998; Dweck, 1999). Thus, feedback will be more helpful and less harmful to students if it targets the task rather than the person.

So, What Does Good Feedback Look Like?
Sadler (1989) identifies three elements of good feedback that are consistent with the aforementioned research and are relevant to the person providing the feedback or the one receiving it:

1) have a clear idea of the standard or reference that is targeted
2) identify the discrepancy between performance and standard
3) take action to address the gap between the two

If attention is placed on the target, on discrepancies between the target and current performance, and on strategies for reducing that discrepancy, the focus properly will be on the *task* rather than the *person*. Furthermore, it is much easier to judge the quality of performance and identify what needs improvement if the target is clear. When teachers connect their feedback to specific standards, student learning improves. Similarly, when students refer to standards when receiving feedback, they are more successful (Sadler, 1989).

Next, attention needs to be given to the gap between desired and actual performance, using the standard or task criteria or rubric as the guide. For example, if a teacher has developed a fairly elaborate rubric as part of a summative assessment on the standard *students will write a persuasive essay*, individual criteria within that rubric can be used to guide practice and feedback of that specific skill.

In addition to such feedback provided by a teacher or media specialist, students can take more ownership of the process by applying task-specific rubrics to their own work, noting areas which need the most improvement.

Similarly, students can compare the expert judgments of educators who completed the rubric with their own judgments, noting and reflecting upon the discrepancies.

Finally, the feedback should help the learner identify strategies for closing the gap. Feedback that targets effort and strategies promotes a more positive attitude toward learning and better performance. Teacher feedback can include examples of more proficient levels of performance, suggestions for new approaches to consider, and questions about why a less appropriate path initially was taken. Again, if students are to learn such skills themselves, we also can ask them to identify suggested improvements, new approaches to the task, and questions they have about what went wrong.

Provide Feedback in a Timely Manner

Summative assessments do not provide feedback about performance when the student most needs it. When students are struggling on a task, they need information about what the gap is and how to fix it right then. Not surprisingly then, immediate feedback is more beneficial than delayed feedback, particularly for tasks that require some thinking (Kulik & Kulik, 1988).

Step 4: Reflection

When students leave our schools, we will not be there at every turn to provide meaningful feedback. They need to learn how to assess their own work. Yet, as Sadler (1989) notes, if we expect students to become proficient at the skill of evaluating their own work they will need to learn the specific skills good self-regulators possess. Most of our students don't leave school with such skills. And our weaker students are even less likely to possess them. As mentioned in Chapter 3, research finds that our poorer students are quite limited in their ability to recognize the weaknesses in their own work (Dunning et al., 2003). Unfortunately, they are also less likely to know how to address their weaknesses even if they could identify them. Hence, our weakest students are less likely to complete Sadler's third element of closing the gap.

Thus, we must engage students in the process of learning by asking them to reflect upon their performance and the feedback they receive about it. That suggests that it is essential to make feedback a dialogue and not just a one-way communiqué.

So, How Can We Promote Good Reflection?

Good reflection should be a natural outgrowth of the feedback process. That is, once students receive feedback concerning the nature of the gap between the standards/criteria and their performance, we should be asking them to consider what they should do with this information. Just as feedback should be a part of a dialogue, remedies for addressing the gap should not simply be fed to the student. Modeling of good strategies for students certainly can benefit them, but if they mindlessly apply those strategies without considering the possibilities themselves, they are unlikely to acquire the aforementioned skills (Sadler, 1989).

- *Develop Self-assessment Skills*
In a chapter on the development and assessment of critical skills, it should not be surprising that one of these critical skills, self-assessment, is an integral part of effective skill development. That is why self-assessment is such a critical skill. We do not want students to become dependent upon educators to judge the quality of their work; it is critical for students to become independent assessors to succeed in the real world.

We need to ask students frequently to identify the standard or criteria relevant to a task, identify the discrepancy between performance and the relevant standard, and take action to address the gap between the two. It is even more critical that we ask the less competent students to do so.

Just through the practice of brief tasks, students will gain valuable information about what is working and not working. Practice provides students with opportunities to discover their strengths and weaknesses that otherwise might be hidden. However, we must also deliberately assign tasks that include an explicit final step in which students are required to evaluate their success, their progress, and the relative effectiveness of different strategies or approaches applied to the task. Again, instead of mindless drill, skill practice can be a thoughtful, student-centered process in which the learner is at least partially responsible for the practice and the formative assessment.

To elaborate on these processes, the following chapters will provide more specific examples of developing and assessing the skills of monitoring one's progress and performance (Chapter 7), information literacy (Chapter 8), and collaboration (Chapter 9).

Assessing the Ability to Monitor One's Progress and Performance   7

At the beginning of Chapter 1, I asked "How many times this week have you stopped to reflect upon a course of action you have taken to determine whether it was working, so that you could make adjustments as needed?" It is an act we engage in frequently, and requires a set of skills that are critical for its success. Its importance is captured quite well in Dunning et al.'s (2003) article previously mentioned. As the authors note, poor performers across intellectual and social domains are also significantly weaker "at spotting the limits of their knowledge and expertise" (p. 83). Weaker writers have difficulty recognizing weaknesses in their writing; weaker readers have trouble knowing if they have extracted the meaning of a text; weaker note-takers often cannot judge if they have captured the essential points of a lecture or reading. So, how are people going to address weaknesses in their performance when they cannot tell there is a problem to be fixed?

Of course, we all struggle at times judging the quality of our work, recognizing when something is well or poorly done, knowing what exactly to look for, and knowing when the work is "finished" for a particular task. All students, not just the weaker ones, need to learn and develop these skills. As described in earlier chapters, the development of such critical skills can be guided by meaningful summative and formative assessments. Thus, in this chapter we will examine some concrete examples of how to assess the ability to monitor one's progress and performance.

It is always useful to first get a clear picture of where you want to end up. So, we will begin by placing monitoring one's progress and performance in the larger context of metacognitive skills so that you have a clearer sense of what we are trying to measure. Then we will be ready to consider some examples of possible summative assessments to measure student demonstration of these skills. Finally, we will explore how you can "plan backwards" from the summative assessments to guide students to the acquisition of these skills through formative assessment.

METACOGNITION

Flavell (1971) introduced the term metacognition to define the knowledge and skills that reflect thinking *about* our thinking. A cognitive (thinking) task would be trying to decide what to make for dinner tonight. A *meta*cognitive act would be realizing that I am not very good at making this type of decision without input from my wife. I am now thinking about my ability to make such decisions. Although no single, agreed upon definition of metacognition has emerged since Flavell (1971) introduced the term, Pintrich, Wolters, and Baxter (2000) effectively described the "general agreement" that metacognition includes three primary components: 1) metacognitive knowledge, 2) metacognitive judgments and monitoring, and 3) self-regulation and control.

Flavell (1979) described "metacognitive knowledge" as comprised of knowledge about the self, knowledge of the tasks one is engaging in, and knowledge of the strategies that can be applied to various tasks. Knowledge of self includes awareness of one's cognitive strengths and weaknesses. For example, I joke with my students that I could more easily remember who they are if I just assigned them numbers; I am much better at remembering numbers than remembering names. Knowledge of tasks includes awareness that certain tasks are more difficult than others and thus require different approaches, or that certain tasks cannot be completed by just one person. Knowledge of strategies includes awareness of how one can best remember, solve problems, read with comprehension, and find information.

Such metacognitive knowledge serves the other two components of metacognition—monitoring and control. As you proceed on a task, you want to be able to *monitor* your performance to remind yourself of the goal(s) and to determine if there is any discrepancy between your performance and the goals. (Readers of Chapter 6 may recognize that this is very similar to elements of good feedback. In essence, monitoring includes self-feedback regarding one's performance.) Good monitoring also includes applying your metacognitive knowledge to the task as you judge whether or not your current strategies are appropriate. Finally, monitoring includes regular judgments of confidence in the correctness of your work, the appropriateness of your strategies, and the degree of progress you are making towards your goals. The less confident you are in your progress, the more likely you should be to reexamine your work and your strategies. We regularly use judgments of confidence as a guide for reappraisal.

If through monitoring you determine sufficient progress is not being made or discrepancies exist between your performance and your goals, you may then adopt new strategies or allocate new resources to better *control* or regulate your performance. Writing these last few paragraphs has required a great deal of metacognition. First, I am aware that I am not a very strong writer. Certainly I cannot just sit down and start writing something coherent. I recognize that creating an outline helps me organize my thoughts. Second, even when I jump into the writing with a clear structure in mind I still frequently encounter frustration over nearly every paragraph I write. Fortunately, I am able to detect in many cases when I am not clearly communicating my ideas. That monitoring leads me to frequently return to a strategy of revisiting the larger idea I am trying to share. I have learned that I am better able to control or regulate my writing when I reexamine my goal(s) for a section, or a paragraph, or even a sentence.

It is remarkable how many metacognitive skills are employed in a single task such as writing or reading or even making dinner. You probably would like your students to acquire all of them. But to make your task as educator manageable, it is often advantageous to deliberately focus on a few critical skills with students. For example, in this chapter, we will examine an approach for the development and assessment of monitoring one's performance or progress. Although one set of skills will be targeted, the approach used to create summative and formative assessments of this set of skills could be applied to any other skill set you would like to develop and measure.

SUMMATIVE ASSESSMENT

So, how would you assess all of the skills involved in monitoring one's progress and performance? You likely would not. To start small (which I often recommend) and to keep the task manageable, target just a few of these skills. Later, if you wanted to broaden the assessments to capture other skills you could. But you want to give sufficient and careful attention to the skills you most want your students to acquire.

First, it is useful to get a complete picture of the metacognitive process you want to assess. Monitoring of one's progress and performance occurs prior to, during, and after a task. Those skills include:

- Thinking about planning and setup for a task
- Assessing how effectively certain strategies are working
- Keeping in mind the nature of a task to ask oneself questions such as, "Will this require much practice?"
- Identifying when to seek external help
- Monitoring personal characteristics such as
    o Motivation level
    o Emotional state
- Monitoring the quality of one's work (i.e., recognizing when one's performance is competent or not)
- Checking one's confidence in how well a task is proceeding

Next, for the sake of focus and space, the latter two sets of skills will be targeted: *Monitoring the competence or quality of one's work* and *checking one's confidence of that quality.* Without the ability to discern the quality of one's work and the degree to which it is meeting the goals of the task, one is unlikely to recognize and attempt to correct the errors or deficiencies.

MONITORING THE QUALITY OF ONE'S WORK

The specific components of effectively monitoring the quality of one's work include skills such as:

- Identifying the goal(s) of the task
- Identifying discrepancies between performance on the task and the goal(s)
- Identifying features of good work on a task
- Recognizing when the task is completed and has met the requirements
- Articulating the strategies for effectively completing the task

CHECKING ONE'S CONFIDENCE IN HOW WELL A TASK IS PROCEEDING

The specific components of effectively checking one's confidence in how well a task is proceeding include skills such as:

- Remembering to occasionally check one's confidence level
- Accurately judging the confidence one should have in how well a task is meeting the requirements or goals

ASSESSING THE MONITORING OF ONE'S PERFORMANCE OR PROGRESS

Since, by definition, these metacognitive or self-regulating skills are occurring in a student's head, how are we to assess them? The strategy described in Chapter 5 for measuring these skills—identifying the observable behavioral indicators of a skill—is not as amenable to measuring someone's thoughts. Thus, researchers and practitioners have relied on methods that ask students to make their thinking visible or ask students to engage in relevant performance-based tasks.

Students have made their metacognitive thinking visible through self-reports, interviews, and think-alouds (Pintrich, Wolters, & Baxter, 2000). In self-reports, students describe after the fact, as best they can, the mental processes they went through in monitoring their performance on some task. Similarly, interviews of students include questions about such processes. Think-alouds, on the other hand, occur during the monitoring of a task as the students talk aloud about the processes they are currently engaging in as they perform the task. A fourth assessment method, performance-based measures, often involves giving students a sample of work to see if they can detect the errors within it as an assessment of whether or not students can monitor the quality of work.

Monitoring the Quality of One's Work

Identifying errors in the work of others seems to be easier than finding them in our own work. However, if a student can find areas of strength and weakness in a sample of someone else's work, it is more likely that he can find it in his own work. So, one approach to assessing the ability to monitor the quality of one's work is to ask students to evaluate the quality of a sample product of some kind. Such an assessment can be created by following the process laid out in Chapter 5: 1) identifying or creating the authentic task, 2) identifying the criteria on which the students' evaluation of the sample will be judged, and 3) designing a rubric to rate the students' work along the criteria. Here are a few examples that could be used with later elementary students.

Paragraph Task 1

Below is a paragraph written to complete the following assignment:

Write a paragraph (with at least four sentences) explaining how you would locate information to produce a report on our solar system. Imagine that a parent is the audience for this paragraph.

Imagine a student wrote the following paragraph in response to the above prompt:

> *(1) To locate information to write a report on our solar system. (2) I would look in the enciclopida. (3) I would ask a librarian there to. (4) This could help, because it has lots of information about different subjects and maybe the book would talk about the animals on earth. (5) I would definately look up the phrase "solar system". (6) Then I would write my report down.*

Answer the following questions about the paragraph:

1) Does sentence #1 effectively communicate the writer's ideas and fit the given assignment? Explain.

2) Does sentence #4 effectively communicate the writer's ideas and fit the given assignment? Explain.

3) Does sentence #5 effectively communicate the writer's ideas and fit the given assignment? Explain.

4) If you could talk to the student who wrote this paragraph, what would you most strongly recommend to improve the paragraph?

Note: The sample paragraph on the previous page represents weak writing skills for a late elementary student. Consequently, it would be easier for the student taking this assessment to find weaknesses in the sample. Thus, such a sample might be appropriate to include in an assessment earlier in the semester or year. At the end of the year, after students have become more proficient at these monitoring skills, a more challenging assessment would include a better written sample in which it would be more difficult to detect discrepancies between performance on the task and the goal.

Possible criteria for Paragraph Task 1 include:

- Effectively identified strengths and weaknesses in selected sentences
- Suggested appropriate focus for improvement of paragraph

Figure 7.1 is a possible rubric (including the bulleted criteria) for scoring performance on Paragraph Task 1.

Figure 7.1 Rubric for Paragraph Task 1

Rubric: Paragraph Task 1				
	Poor	**Fair**	**Good**	**Excellent**
Criteria				
Did the student effectively identify the strengths and weaknesses of sentence #1?	No, not at all	Only for one or two of the strengths and weaknesses	Yes, for most of the strengths and weaknesses	Yes
For sentence #1, did the student identify whether or not the paragraph fit the assignment?	No, not at all		Yes, but not completely accurately	Yes, very effectively
Did the student effectively identify the strengths and weaknesses of sentence #4?	No, not at all	Only for one or two of the strengths and weaknesses	Yes, for most of the strengths and weaknesses	Yes
For sentence #4, did the student identify whether or not the paragraph fit the assignment?	No, not at all		Yes, but not completely accurately	Yes

Rubric: Paragraph Task 1 continued				
	Poor	**Fair**	**Good**	**Excellent**
Criteria				
Did the student effectively identify the strengths and weaknesses of sentence #5?	No, not at all	Only for one or two of the strengths and weaknesses	Yes, for most of the strengths and weaknesses	Yes
For sentence #5, did the student identify whether or not the paragraph fit the assignment?	No, not at all		Yes, but not completely accurately	Yes
Did the student suggest an appropriate focus for improvement of work?	No, failed to suggest any reasonable improvement	Yes, but suggested a less important focus for improvement (e.g., fix spelling errors)	Yes, suggested appropriate focus for improvement but without clearly connecting to purpose of assignment	Yes, suggested appropriate focus for improvement clearly connected to purpose of assignment

Note: *Obviously, point values could be assigned to the rubric for grading purposes. Likely, each criterion above would be weighted equally.*

To thoroughly assess standards, assessments should be multiple and varied. For example, Paragraph Task 1 primarily focuses on the recognition of quality in individual sentences within a paragraph, while Paragraph Task 2 that follows, using a similar format, assesses students' more holistic evaluation of a sample of writing. As a result, the paragraph tasks address an overlapping but varied set of monitoring skills:

Paragraph Task 1: Students will:

- Identify discrepancies between performance on the task and the goal(s)
- Identify features of good work on a task

Paragraph Task 2: Students will:

- Identify the goal(s) of the task
- Identify discrepancies between performance on the task and the goal(s)
- Recognize when the task is completed and has met the requirements

Paragraph Task 2

Imagine that students were assigned to write a paragraph which explained how to complete a simple task. The assignment said to include all the steps for completing the task. In response to the assignment, one student wrote the following paragraph:

When I play soccer I like to play goalie. The goalie gets to stop the shots the other team kicks. I like to pretend that I am guarding a cave and I can't let anything in it. Also, I get to wear special gloves that are for the goalie.

Answer the following questions about the assignment and the student's paragraph.

1) What is the main goal of the paragraph assignment?

2) How well does the student's paragraph meet the goal you listed above? Circle one:

   doesn't meet goal at all   somewhat meets goal   meets goal well

3) Explain how the student's paragraph does or does not meet the goal you listed above.

4) For this question, ignore the quality of the writing in the paragraph. Just answer: Has the writer of the paragraph met all of the requirements of the assignment? Circle one:

   Yes   No

5) If you said "No," describe which requirements are not yet met by the student's paragraph.

As an alternative to the more detailed analytic rubric presented for Paragraph Task 1, a simpler holistic rubric, illustrated in Figure 7.2, could be used to evaluate students' answers to the questions for Paragraph Task 2.

Figure 7.2 Rubric for Paragraph Task 2

Rubric: Paragraph Task 2

Limited: Did not identify the main goal of the assignment and did not say how the paragraph missed the goal

Progressing: Started to explain whether the paragraph did or did not meet the goal, but still some confusion about the goal and how the paragraph might have missed the assigned topic

Proficient: Clearly identified the goal and whether or not the requirements were met, but still a little confusion about how the paragraph might have missed the goal of the assignment

Exemplary: Effectively described the goal, whether or not the requirements were met, and how the paragraph might have missed the main goal of the assignment

Note: Rubrics for both paragraph tasks were written generically enough so that they could be applied to any type of sample of work, not just a sample of writing. For example, in the Paragraph Task 1, any specific element of a sample of work (e.g., a line in a musical composition or performance, a step or steps in a problem solution) could be substituted for "sentence" in the criteria for that task. So, the assessments in the Paragraph Tasks, or some variation of them, could be administered in any classroom or lab or media center for any sample of work in any subject.

Identifying Features of Good Work

To more specifically assess whether or not students can identify features of good work on a task and, consequently, know what they should be monitoring, you can ask them directly.

What Does Good Work Look Like?

Present students with an example of an assignment relevant to their coursework. It could be a research paper assignment, an oral presentation assignment, a lab report assignment, or an assignment asking students to construct a model, solve a problem, create a marketing brochure, or compare and contrast cultures.

Ask questions such as the following:

1) What needs to be included in this assignment for it to be completed?
2) What characteristics should a good persuasive essay (or substitute any type of task such as a lab report, choral performance, or floor plan) possess?
3) If you were to work on this task, how could you tell if you were doing a good job as you worked on your essay?
4) If you completed this assignment, how could you tell if you had written a good persuasive essay when you were done?

As you likely know, it can be sobering to discover what students believe is needed to complete an assignment or what good work on a task would look like. Yet, it can be informative for students to think about what good performance on a task looks like before they begin a task. That is why tasks such as *What Does Good Work Look Like?* may better serve as formative rather than summative assessments as I will discuss below.

Furthermore, although the tasks can give us some information about how well a student can identify strengths and weaknesses in a sample of work, it does not necessarily tell us if a student is *actively monitoring his own work* to identify such strengths and weaknesses. In other words, like most assessments, the tasks provide us with some but not all the evidence we would need to evaluate a student's monitoring skills.

Actively Monitoring One's Own Work

To determine if students are even aware that monitoring would be useful and how it should occur, an authentic task could be accompanied by a survey or interview of students about their monitoring. For example, after students have completed an assignment, many teachers ask students to *reflect* upon their work in a variety of ways (Step 4 of good skill development). Such reflection can include a review of what processes they engaged in as they were completing the assignment. (Again, I am not talking about the strategies students employed to *produce* quality work. I am separating those cognitive skills of self-regulation and control from the skills of monitoring. That separation is somewhat artificial, but it is feasible for the purpose of assessment.)

For example, after students have completed an assignment, ask them to complete the following reflection journal entry.

Reflection Journal

Answer the following questions regarding the _____ assignment you just completed:

1) How did you check on your progress as you worked on this assignment?

2) How did you make sure you were doing a good job on the assignment?

3) How did you make sure you were completing the assignment successfully?

4) What should a person do while working on an assignment like this one to make sure his work is of good quality?

5) What do you do while working on an assignment like this one to make sure your work is of good quality?

6) On this assignment, could you tell if you were doing a good or poor job while you were working on it? Circle one:

Yes   No

7) If you said "Yes," how were you able to tell how well you were doing on the assignment?

Note: You would likely ask only one to three such questions for a reflective assignment, but I have included others to illustrate a variety of ways you can assess these monitoring skills.

Assessing student monitoring in real time, as researchers have done with think-alouds, may be prohibitively time consuming in most classrooms or libraries. However, briefer versions of this approach could be accomplished by stopping a group of students as they work on an assignment and asking them to briefly answer a question similar to those in the *Reflection Journal* task. It may be uniquely informative to capture such reflection as a task is proceeding.

Checking One's Confidence in How Well a Task Is Proceeding
If students feel quite confident in their performance on a task they are less likely to review that performance to see if it can be improved. Unfortunately, most students, and particularly the weaker ones, are not consistently accurate in their judgments of confidence. Consequently, students might conclude that an assignment is completed or well done and needs no further consideration when it actually is a weak effort. That is why remembering to check one's confidence about progress on a task and accurately judging one's confidence are critical skills in the process of monitoring one's progress and performance.

To assess these skills students could be asked to complete a variety of tasks. First, to see if students even recognize that stopping to check their confidence is an important step, you can simply quiz them on what are important steps in the process of completing an assignment.

What Should You Do?

Put a check mark next to the actions listed below that you think are important to take as you complete work such as the _____ assignment.

1) Ask others how they are approaching the assignment.
2) Review the requirements of the assignment occasionally.
3) Create two or more complete versions of the assignment and then choose the one that is best.
4) Stop and ask yourself along the way how confident you are that what you just did is well done or meets the requirements of the assignment.
5) Occasionally evaluate the strategies you are using to determine if they are effective.
6) Take frequent breaks.
7) Start creating your product right away so you get some ideas out there and then go back and organize your work.
8) Don't start too early on the assignment or you might forget what you had done earlier.
9) Drink plenty of fluids.
10) Stop and review your work occasionally to make sure it is of sufficient quality.

For action #4 in the list, briefly explain why you said that was or was not an important step to take in completing the assignment.

Note: This is not a complete list of possible actions someone might take while working on an assignment by any means, but it provides a sample of what you might present to students to check their meta-cognitive knowledge for completing assignments.

To find out if students are actually stopping to check their confidence in the quality of their work while completing a task, you could ask one or more of the questions in the *Reflection Journal* task. To determine if students are *accurately* judging their confidence you could simply ask them to assess their level of confidence in their work during or after completion of an assignment. You could then collect students' work and compare it against their judgments of confidence. This could be measured by asking students to put a number from 0-100 (representing a percentage) on the top of an assignment when they are turning it in indicating their level of confidence that it successfully met the requirements of the assignment. Or, you could ask them to put a score on top of the assignment as a prediction of what score they believe they will receive on the task. You can then quickly compare their judgment with their actual performance.

Of course, improving students' accuracy in judging the confidence in their work is in one sense just a means to an end, the end of successfully completing an assignment. So, assessing students' accuracy in judging their confidence may better serve as a formative assessment that is embedded in the instruction of other skills, as I will discuss in the next section. On the other hand, you might understandably view this monitoring skill as so critical that you want to summatively assess it as well to confirm that students have acquired this valuable skill.

Beyond Elementary Grades

The previous assessments were designed with late elementary students in mind. However, each of them easily could be adapted for middle school, high school, or even college students. In fact, many of the same questions listed in the *What Should You Do?* task could be used while only the complexity or difficulty of the task increases.

For example, in the introductory psychology course I teach at North Central College I could ask my students to review a sample of their own work or a sample I give them and reflect upon their monitoring skills. Certainly, my students have not yet mastered those abilities. I currently choose to assess some other critical skills in that course instead, but I regularly see how critical effective monitoring is to the success of my students as the weaker ones visit my office surprised by the low grade they received or the difficulty a particular assignment is giving them.

FORMATIVE ASSESSMENT

Although some students struggle with the ability to monitor their own progress while reading a text or preparing for a test or writing a paper, the importance of effectively monitoring performance, and even what actions are important in that process, have been mentioned or taught to many of them at some time in the past. The problem, as repeated throughout this text, is that we typically do not teach these critical skills in a careful, *systematic* manner and that we do not assess the skills to determine if students have acquired them.

To effectively teach such skills, the skills need to be formatively assessed on a frequent basis (Black & Wiliam, 1998). That is, as described in Chapter 6, students need to be given numerous opportunities to practice a skill, receive meaningful and timely feedback, and reflect upon their progress. Teachers can check for understanding during this process and make adjustments in instruction.

This chapter began with a focus on summative assessment of these skills because as stated before: The end is the place to begin. Similarly, knowing what your summative assessments look like can guide the development of your instruction and formative assessment of these skills.

CHECKING ONE'S CONFIDENCE IN HOW WELL A TASK IS PROCEEDING

If we consider the skill of accurately judging the confidence one should have in the quality of one's work, the measure of comparing a student's judgment of confidence versus the student's actual performance (as a summative assessment) can be used as a check to guide development of disciplinary knowledge and skills as well as the development of this monitoring skill.

Example: High School Science Class

Consider a high school science class. Students are assigned to write a research report on some topic. They are using the school's library media center to access electronic and print resources for reference. The classroom teacher is collaborating with a media specialist to teach the students both the research skills necessary to find useful information and the monitoring skills.

For example, as students first frame a question to be investigated, the teacher or media specialist can ask the students to turn in their question along with a judgment of confidence in the likelihood that their question is an appropriate one. Brief feedback is given on the quality of the question, in oral or written form. Additionally, a sample of students (it does not have to be all of them every time) is also given feedback, oral or written, about why their confidence rating does or does not match their performance.

Such a conversation about a possible discrepancy between confidence and performance allows the educators to 1) further instruct students about framing a good question (here is why you should not have been so confident) and 2) further instruct students about how to make more accurate judgments of confidence (here is what you need to consider in judging your confidence level). This latter instruction could include asking the students why they think their judgments of confidence were a little or a lot off base.

Certainly, a single opportunity to reflect upon one's confidence judgment is not sufficient to learn such a skill. So, later on in the same task the media specialist could ask a sample of students to rate how confident they were that they had selected appropriate sources to access information for their reports. Once again, feedback and conversation could take place around the accuracy of the students' judgments. That could include further instruction on how to increase accuracy and, presumably, confidence in their judgments.

Since these are formative assessments intended to check and further understanding of the students, no grading is required. Instead, quick, informal comments, oral or written, can be provided to students. Yet, these formative assessments do provide the educators information about how well students are developing the complementary skills of researching a topic and judging how well they are completing that task. The educators can then adjust instruction of each accordingly.

The teacher or media specialist can ask for confidence judgments at any step in this process. Perhaps students would be required to write a brief journal entry at the end of the process about their final level of confidence, and why they have that level of confidence, as evidence of and an opportunity for reflection.

In skill development, it is often most effective to begin with simple, small steps and build toward more complex and integrated versions of the skill. Yet, repetition is critical. Throughout a semester or year students should be given many opportunities to rate their confidence in their work, receive prompt feedback on their ratings, engage in discussion about how to make more accurate judgments, and, finally, articulate the strategies that make up this critical skill.

MONITORING THE QUALITY OF ONE'S WORK

To illustrate how formative assessment can be used to develop another critical monitoring skill, let's look at a few examples of formatively assessing a student's ability to judge whether or not their current work is proceeding well. For any educator who wants to develop critical monitoring skills, I would recommend the following tasks for any grade for any subject.

Example: Middle School Math Class

Consider a middle school math class. Students are preparing for an upcoming quiz or exam. Do they know when they are ready? Can they recognize any discrepancy between the goal of being prepared for the test and their actual readiness? Unfortunately, many students are not very good at this fairly difficult skill. Yet, it is a critical one. Not only will these students need to make this judgment for countless tests in their future, but they will need this skill later in life when judging if they are ready to give a presentation or teach a lesson, or ready to compete in a marathon, or ready to buy a house. How will they know?

So, along with preparing students for the next test, educators can also prepare them to become better monitors of their readiness for a task. How might you do this? As discussed in previous chapters, it will take lots of practice with more sophisticated practice building on simple first attempts.

The following is one possible approach:

- Start the semester with some conversation about what students believe are effective strategies for judging readiness.
- The teacher can engage in some early instruction by commenting on the effectiveness of some of these strategies or asking students why they think certain strategies would be more or less effective.
- Soon after this initial discussion the teacher could assign a brief one or two question quiz for the next day covering a narrow topic. Ask students to use one or more of the strategies discussed or one of their own strategies to judge if they are ready before they stop studying.
- The next day, before they take the quiz, ask students to write down the strategy(ies) they used. Also ask them to rate how confident they are about their performance on the quiz: Not at all confident, somewhat confident, or very confident.

As the semester proceeds, you would repeat this process with increasingly more substantial quizzes and exams. To accompany the practice, students will also need good feedback from peers and educators about the discrepancies between their perceived readiness and their actual readiness. Such feedback can and should be delivered in a variety of ways. This can include occasional brief one-on-one conversations with students, particularly for those who are more consistently inaccurate in their judgments of readiness. Educators can also engage the class as a whole on what they are finding to be effective and ineffective strategies. Obviously, those who struggle with judging readiness often do so because they also struggle conceptually with the subject matter. So, conversation about discrepancies in perceived and actual readiness will often necessitate discussion of discrepancies in perceived and actual understanding of subject matter, which should further benefit the weaker students. As can frequently be seen in the development of these critical skills, skill development can and should intertwine with the development of students' grasp of the concepts.

Another formative assessment would be to have students pair up to quiz each other before an upcoming test. Each partner could make a series of judgments of readiness of the other member of the pair, sharing that judgment and the reasons why. As the teacher circulates around the room, occasionally providing feedback or asking questions, the pairs continue to review and practice with each other, hopefully until each partner is confident in his own and his partner's readiness for the exam.

Example: Elementary Language Arts

Finally, to return to the skill of judging the quality of one's work as captured by the summative paragraph tasks and the *What Does Good Work Look Like?* task, consider a classroom in which the process of writing is being taught. Whether the current focus is on a five-paragraph persuasive essay or fiction writing or writing a newspaper column, such instruction can be intertwined with instruction and formative assessment of the monitoring of the quality of one's ongoing progress and performance.

Each step of the writing process can and should be formatively assessed as students are given ample practice and feedback. That same formative assessment of students' ability to engage in editing a draft or pre-writing tasks such as outlining can also include questions addressing students' monitoring skills. For example:

- How do you know your outline is complete? Or that your points are in a logical order?
- What did you do (could you do) to check to see if your outline has a logical flow to it?
- How will you know if you have found all the mechanical errors in your draft?
- Should you check to see if your draft meets the task requirements? Why or why not?
- What were you trying to say with your first sentence? How do you know that readers will interpret it in that same way?
- How confident are you that your piece is written for the appropriate audience? Why?

Perhaps before students are ready to answer such questions about their own work, an educator can display other samples of work for the entire class and model the process of checking one's progress. Teacher and students can identify and discuss the relative merits of different strategies or ideas.

In addition to formatively assessing students with such questions or exercises, you can also stop students in the middle of their work on occasion and ask them to reflect on their progress. "How's it going?" "Fine." That is how students (and adults) will often respond to such a vague query. If we really want to know about their progress, their confidence, and their confusion, we have to draw out those responses in a more deliberate manner.

For example, it can be quite enlightening (and frustrating or rewarding) to discover how someone else interprets your writing. So, stop your students in the middle of their work and pair them up. Ask each partner to read part or all of what the other student has written so far. The partner then describes what she believes the writer is trying to communicate. "Ouch!" Or, "Exactly!" The two students then discuss why there was or was not a discrepancy between the writer's intent and the reader's interpretation. Additionally, the partners can be asked to discuss how the writer might better judge how the text will be interpreted. Presumably, you would have already provided some instruction and practice in such skills.

As you know, tasks that require students to reveal their unfinished (or finished) work to their peers can be threatening for many students. However, it will not be nearly as uncomfortable if this is done on a regular rather than infrequent basis in your classroom or media center. Additionally, I refer you to Carol Dweck's work (e.g., Dweck, 1999; Dweck, 2006; Dweck & Molden, 2005), mentioned in Chapter 6, which finds that students are more likely to persist and seek out such challenges rather than be threatened by them if they are taught that their abilities are malleable and not fixed, and if they are praised primarily for their effort and the strategies they choose rather than their performance.

IN SUMMARY

To most effectively assess students' skill development, whether summatively or formatively, you want to be very clear about which specific skills you are teaching and measuring. Do not just say you are assessing monitoring skills and occasionally ask some of the questions discussed in this chapter. Students will be confused about the purpose of the instruction, and you will not be able to definitively assess their progress on the skills.

To be more effective, identify two to five specific skills which make up monitoring (or any other skill you want to develop) and teach and track those specific skills systematically. That is, begin by giving your students brief tasks that isolate one of those subskills, giving students plenty of opportunity to practice the skill, receive feedback on it, and reflect upon their progress. Then, continue to provide opportunities for students to practice each skill in gradually more complex contexts or forms, eventually assigning tasks that require students to apply more than one of the subskills. Some of these tasks may be embedded assessments that you grade, and others may simply be ungraded opportunities for practice.

Does this process of teaching and assessing monitoring skills consume a little more of your valuable class time? Yes. Is it worth it? That is something you have to decide. I have been making the point that students will be much better prepared for many of the everyday tasks they will encounter in school, work, and life as a result of developing such critical skills. Students who acquire such monitoring skills are also learning to self-assess, to become less dependent upon the judgment of others, and more capable of and confident in

Assessing Information Literacy Skills

8

How many times did you Google something this week? Or, search some newspaper archives? Or, want to know another word for "synonym"? Finding useful information has become critical to work, school, and life. As mentioned in Chapter 3, surveys of employers and studies of the workplace regularly identify information literacy as an essential skill for the 21st century. (And it was pretty useful in that last century, too!) As technologically savvy as our children might be right now, it does not mean they know how to find and evaluate information. We are not born information literate. Like any skill, it requires significant instruction and modeling, practice, feedback, and reflection. As described throughout this text, those skill-building processes are significantly enhanced through summative and formative assessment.

INFORMATION LITERACY

The American Library Association (ALA) defines information literacy as follows: "To be information literate, a person must be able to recognize when information is needed and have the ability to locate, evaluate, and use effectively the needed information. The information literate individuals are those who have learned how to learn" (ALA, 1989). As opposed to the meta-cognitive skill of monitoring addressed in Chapter 7, information literacy skills have been well articulated, deliberately taught, and frequently assessed. For example, as many of you know, AASL and ACRL have created well-defined sets of standards for information literacy.

Regarding assessment, Neely and her co-authors (2006) offer a variety of information literacy assessment efforts and tools, including one chapter for each of the five ACRL standards. Additionally, they list more than 70 assessment tools in the appendix that others have created. Avery (2003) offers stories of the development of a large variety of assessments by college librarians and their colleagues, including the complete assessments and rubrics developed. Similarly, Harada and Yoshina (2005) offer a considerable variety of assessment ideas for the K-12 environment, including many for younger students. In other words, librarians and media specialists have had some success in engaging classroom teachers in the process of developing general and discipline-specific measures of information literacy. However, there is still a great deal of work to be done to integrate these essential skills throughout school curricula. So, offered in this chapter are some assessment tasks and rubrics to add to a growing library of resources for measuring these valuable skills.

To provide a framework for the following examples, I am selecting a subset of standards of information literacy found in the AASL standards, or the ACRL standards, or most lists of such outcomes (e.g., The Big6). I am limiting my definition of information literacy to "finding useful information." To unpack that three word definition, I would begin by stating that before someone can find *useful* information, one has to know for what it will be used. In other words, as described in other sets of standards, the searcher must be able to define a question or a need for information. Then one needs to know where to best find information that will answer the question, be able to access the needed information from those sources, determine if the accessed information is useful in answering the question, and, finally, recognize when enough good information has been acquired to answer the question.

The target set of skills addressed in this chapter are the ones described earlier in Chapter 2. Specifically, to be information literate, one needs to be able to:

- Define or frame a question to be answered
- Locate appropriate sources of information that address the question
- Access the information from a variety of electronic and non-electronic sources
- Evaluate the accuracy, relevancy, authority, and currency of the information for the question
- Determine when sufficient information has been acquired to answer the question

I am intentionally excluding a standard for *using* the information once it has been located, accessed, and evaluated. Virtually everything we do involves using information, so, in my view, to include it in the definition of information literacy unnecessarily broadens it. If I look up a recipe for steak tartare, and use that information to prepare it, and my wife walks into the kitchen at that moment, I am not going to say, "Look, dear, I'm engaging in information literacy!" (Believe me, I have tried it; you get a weird look.) No, we already have a name for that act—preparing steak tartare. (Full disclosure: I actually have no idea what steak tartare is; I just like the sound of it. Maybe I should look it up!)

More seriously, *communicating the information*, which is included in many sets of information literacy standards already, is defined in standards of writing and speaking. I believe to include such *uses* of information dilutes the meaning of information literacy, stretching it too far.

Of course, that is just my preference, and I am intentionally constraining the set of standards to simplify the illustration. Fortunately, you should be able to adapt the examples of summative and formative assessment to whatever set of information literacy skills you prefer.

SUMMATIVE ASSESSMENT

Upon perusing Avery's (2003), Harada and Yoshina's (2005), and Neely's (2006) surveys of information literacy assessments, two things become apparent. First, librarians and their colleagues have developed quite a variety of tools to assess information literacy. Second, librarians recognize that information literacy includes knowledge *and* skills. Thus, it makes sense that many summative assessments of information literacy are a blend of forced-choice items and performance tasks. As already established, multiple-choice items are more efficient tools for collecting student data, and are more effective measures for assessing student knowledge (Haladyna, 1999). On the other hand, authentic assessments more directly capture meaningful application of information literacy skills. Combining the two can create a meaningful and manageable assessment of information literacy.

For example, The Bay Area Community Colleges Information Competency Assessment Project developed an excellent test that includes 47 forced-choice items and 12 performance-based exercises (see the Project at <http://www.topsy.org/ICAP/ICAProject.html>). The assessment was carefully aligned with specific standards, and performance on the exercises is measured through detailed rubrics. As a result, librarians and faculty at community colleges in the San Francisco area have an effective tool for identifying strengths and weaknesses in their students' information literacy skills and to measure progress in their growth.

FORCED-CHOICE MEASURES

Quite a few examples of forced-choice measures can be found online (see a list at <http://jonathan.mueller.faculty.noctrl.edu/infolitassessments.htm>) and elsewhere. Some of them, such as TRAILS (Tool for Real-Time Assessment of Information Literacy Skills, <http://trails-9.org/index.php>), which is available at no cost to library media specialists and teachers, are automated so they can be completed online. Some primarily address knowledge in Bloom's taxonomy of cognitive objectives (1956) while other quizzes assess comprehension, application, and analysis through the use of scenarios. A number of detailed guides for constructing good tests are available as well (e.g., Mueller, 2006). Given the plethora of resources for forced-choices tests, I will focus on examples of performance tasks in this chapter that could serve as standalone assessments or could be combined with some forced-choice questions.

AUTHENTIC MEASURES

Authentic assessment of information literacy has taken many forms from webliographies to portfolios to journals to research projects to hands-on searches. (See a list of many possible assessment tasks at <http://www.library.cqu.edu.au/services/staff-research/infolit/teaching/assess-list.htm>.) Some of these tasks target individual skills while others assess more comprehensive integration of the skills in a larger project.

Individual Skills

Although information seeking is commonly a process involving multiple tasks and skills, it is still possible to isolate and assess individual skills within information literacy for summative purposes. Is a student capable of locating appropriate sources? This can be effectively assessed at the end of a unit, or a semester, or a year through simple tasks such as those I will describe in this chapter. Then, such individual assessments of specific skills can, in conjunction with a more complex task that incorporates locating sources, serve to determine if a student has met that particular information literacy standard or outcome.

The following three approaches (scenarios, research logs, hands-on searches) work particularly well for directly measuring one or more skills. Moreover, because so many good examples of these tasks have been created, I will supplement my examples with already existing measures to illustrate the process of assessing information literacy.

Scenarios

In this type of task, students are presented with an imaginary search to conduct and asked how they would conduct it, usually through a series of questions.

• *Framing a Search Question*

For example, to assess framing a search question, students could be given the following task:

Task

Forming a research question from a broad topic

Let's say that you wanted to research the topic "computer and Internet crimes." Given that broad area of interest, what might be a research question to investigate—for example, "Should governments get involved in regulating use of the Internet?"

With permission from *Information Literacy Assessment*, at <http://www.topsy.org/InfoLitAssess.html>

Or, a student in elementary school could be asked:

Task
Imagine that you are interested in nutrition and vitamins. Write a specific question you could research that is related to that topic.

A *rubric* that could accompany either of the *Framing a Search Question* assessment tasks is illustrated in Figure 8.1.

Figure 8.1: Rubric for Framing a Research Question

Framing a Research Question Rubric			
Criteria	Limited	Adequate	Proficient
Narrows topic	Research question remains vague or excessively broad or narrow	Research question has been narrowed to a fairly decipherable and manageable topic	Research question is appropriately specific and coherently defined
Question within scope of original topic	Research question primarily falls outside of original topic	Although the research question does not lie completely within original topic, it is sufficiently related	Research question clearly falls within general scope

Here is a rubric for the *Framing a Search Question* assessment tasks written at the elementary level.

Figure 8.2: Rubric for Framing a Research Question (Elementary Version)

Framing a Research Question Rubric			
Criteria	Limited	Adequate	Proficient
Specific topic	The research question is unclear or is too broad or narrow	The research question is fairly specific and understandable	The research question is appropriately specific and clearly defined
Question fits original topic	The research question does not fit the topic given	Although the research question does not completely fit the topic, it is sufficiently related	The research question clearly fits the original topic

- *Evaluating the Information and Source*

To assess the skill of evaluating the accuracy, relevancy, authority, and currency of the information for the question, you could ask:

Figure 8.3 is a rubric to apply to the *Evaluating the Information and Source* task:

Figure 8.3: Rubric for Evaluating a Source

Evaluating a Source Rubric			
Criteria	**Poor**	**Good**	**Excellent**
How to check for accuracy	Incomplete or inaccurate explanation	Identifies strategies that would permit some but not strong confidence in source	Identifies best strategies for checking validity of claims/facts
How to check for relevancy	Incomplete or inaccurate explanation	Identifies some appropriate means for comparing source to question	Identifies effective process for checking relevancy to question
How to check for authority	Incomplete or inaccurate explanation	Identifies some but not always best strategies for checking authority	Describes how to identify and evaluate authority of source
How to check for currency	Incomplete or inaccurate explanation	Identifies some but not all primary clues for currency	Identifies best places to check for currency of source

Or, if you wanted to see if students know what criteria to apply, you could ask them to evaluate one or more sites *without* naming the criteria they should apply.

Another example for older students:

> ## Task
>
> Study the following citation to an article, and in your own words describe if and how the citation approaches the criteria listed below:
>
> Levy, Elliot, S., Patricia M. Flynn, Diane M Kellog. 1999. Balancing professional and personal lives: The mantra for the next millennium. *CPA Journal* 69 (10): 70-73.
>
> 1) Is this a reliable or trustworthy source? Why or why not?
> 2) Is this a valid or reputable study? Why or why not?
> 3) Would you say this source is likely to be accurate? Why or why not?
> 4) Can you construe the authority of the authors? How or how not?
> 5) Is this a timely source? Why or why not?
> 6) What would the likelihood of bias be, if any, with a source such as this? Why or why not?

With permission from Ann Fiegen and Bennett Cherry, *Pre-Test/Post-Test Assessment*, California State University, San Marcos

For a younger audience you might ask:

> ## Task
>
> Imagine that while searching for information on . . . you came across a book called . . . Describe three things you could check in the book to find out if it is a reliable source of information for your topic. (Optionally, you also could ask students to tell you *why* they picked those three things to check.)

Another good type of constructed-response assessment is to present students with the real or imagined work of another student and ask them to critique it in terms of the skills being assessed. For example:

Task

Imagine that Steve was looking for information about "the size of the planets in our solar system." He found a book called *Our Solar System*. Steve decided it would be a good source of information for his topic because the book:

- Was about our solar system
- Had lots of pictures of planets
- Included an index

Question 1: Was Steve correct in deciding that the book would be a good source for his topic? Why or why not?

Question 2: What else in the book could Steve have checked to determine if it was a good source for his topic?

Figure 8.4 is a rubric to apply to the evaluating sources task.

Figure 8.4: Rubric for Identifying Characteristics of a Good Source

Identifying Characteristics of a Good Source Rubric				
Criteria	**Poor (0)**	**Good (3)**	**Excellent (5)**	**Weighting**
Q1: Was Steve correct?	Answer did not accurately evaluate Steve's clues	Accurately evaluated relevancy of 2 of the clues	Effectively evaluated relevancy of clues	X2
Q2: What else could Steve have checked?	Did not identify any appropriate clue OR identified an irrelevant clue		Identified at least one appropriate clue and no irrelevant ones	

Note: As discussed in Chapter 5, you are not required to assign an equal number of levels of performance to each criterion in a rubric. Thus, while responses to Q1 are being judged across three levels in the above rubric, responses to Q2 can be judged as meeting or failing to meet the criterion.

- *Accessing the Information*

The following task could be adapted to assess this skill in a variety of ways for a variety of ages:

Use Boolean operators, phrase searching, and truncation to translate the search topics in 3-1 through 3-5 into search commands for Infotrac Expanded Academic Index.

3-1. statistics on teen pregnancy

_____

3-2. defaults on student loans

_____

3-3. racial profiling by police

_____

3-4. effects of irrigation on the Colorado River

_____

3-5. stem cells in the treatment of diseases

_____

With permission from *ENGL 101 Information Literacy Assessment Post-Test,* Dakota State University

The Research Log

Instead of an imaginary search to conduct, students can be given a real task to perform. After or during the search, in a research log or journal, students are sometimes required to describe certain steps they completed in their information search or answer questions about it (e.g., "What keywords did you use?"). Again, a series of questions can be asked about the entire process, or questions can be asked about one or two steps in the process. For example, to assess evaluation of sources:

Imagine that you are researching melatonin and find the three Web pages listed below. Visit each site. Then pick two of them and in two or three sentences evaluate each according to standard evaluation criteria. Be as specific as possible.

URL </www.priory.com/mel.htm>
URL <www.fda.gov/fdac/features/1998/498_sleep.html>
URL <www.aafp.org/afp/971001ap/cupp.html>

Evaluation of site 1
    Identify the Web site:
    Your evaluation:
Evaluation of site 2
    Identify the Web site:
    Your evaluation:

With permission from the *Bay Area Community Colleges Information Competency Assessment Project*

Hands-on Search

In this task, students are presented with a search to conduct. As they conduct the search, the students' performance is observed and recorded. For example, in a *Library Media Connection* article (Mueller, 2005), I described an assessment used by the library media specialists at Lockport Township High School. Library staff at Lockport teamed with classroom teachers to turn a typical research paper assignment into an information literacy assessment. Information about student performance was gathered before, during, and after searching, as captured by the information fluency rubric in Figure 8.5. Because the purpose of their assessment was to measure school progress in developing these skills rather than on individual performance, the librarians were able to randomly select only a few students to monitor through the search process. That made a rather labor-intensive assessment process more manageable.

Figure 8.5: Rubric for Assessing Information Fluency

Information Fluency Rubric				
	4	**3**	**2**	**1**
Thesis Statement	Fully developed thesis statement	Partially developed thesis statement	Topic ideas included, little to no development	No thesis statement developed
Research Preparation	Developed a defined task list, outline or other organization tool of resource information needed	Partial task list, outline or other organizational tool of resource information needed	Vague list of information needed	No organizational tool generated
Utilization of Electronic Catalog and Databases	Utilized electronic catalog and/ or electronic databases Located journals, books, or other print sources to use for research	Utilized electronic catalog and/ or electronic databases Found few resources	Utilized electronic catalog and/or electronic databases Found no resources	Did not use electronic catalog and/or electronic databases
Seeking Assistance	Asked insightful questions of others to help utilize sources available	Asked others for help to find sources	Asked others for the information they found instead of finding it themselves	Did not ask anyone for information or help when needed

Information Fluency Rubric				
	4	**3**	**2**	**1**
Reference Books	Used a variety of reference books to locate information	Used general reference books to locate information	Copied information from reference books	Did not use reference books
Internet Research Skills	Utilized 4 or more electronic databases such as ProQuest, and Encyclopedia Britannica on MIS site or other informative research sites such as Library of Congress archives, used concise keywords to narrow down research choices	Utilized 3 electronic databases such as ProQuest, and Encyclopedia Britannica on MIS site or other informative research sites such as Library of Congress archives	Utilized 2 or fewer electronic databases on MIS site or 2 or fewer other informative research sites	Utilized search engines only
Resources Found	Found 5 or more quality and varied reference sources including electronic and printed material	Found 3 or less quality and reference sources. All sources were of the same type (printed material or electronic, etc.)	Found 1 reference source	Found 0 reference sources
Analyzing Information	Read entire segments, journal articles, or Web sources, summarized key information for project	Skimmed resources and summarized information for project	Notes include a combination of plagiarized and original material	Plagiarized information from sources
Note-Taking Skills	Followed organization tool such as outline or task list, jotting notes from sources and citing sources	Randomly jotted down notes from sources	Marked important information, did not jot notes	Did not take notes

continued on next page

Information Fluency Rubric				
	4	**3**	**2**	**1**
Work Cited	Used standard MLA format for work cited, including graphics and electronic sources	Used standard MLA format for work cited Did not include electronic sources	Briefly listed titles of sources and some other information	Did not cite sources

With permission from Lockport Township High School, Lockport, IL

Again, instead of assessing all of the components of the information fluency rubric in one task, alternatively you could observe student performance on just one or two of the individual skills. Similarly, students could be asked to perform one or more of these steps as part of a larger, blended assessment that also included some forced-choice items.

FORMATIVE ASSESSMENT

This section will be rather short because, by now, you probably recognize that the brief summative assessments described in the previous section can also serve as formative assessments during the instruction and practice steps of skill building. Furthermore, the embedding of information literacy instruction and formative assessment within the curriculum should not just take place in language arts classes or library instruction. As with the development of all the skills described in this text, information literacy can and should be taught in all the disciplines.

EXAMPLE: ELEMENTARY SCHOOL SCIENCE

Embedded in a fourth-grade assignment to learn about sources of air pollution and finding ways to reduce it in one's community, students can be asked to define a specific question they intend to investigate. The classroom teacher or library media specialist could engage the class in some comparison of different questions students created to provide feedback and encourage reflection on this skill.

Or, a separate activity could precede the air pollution project in which students practice refining fairly nebulous questions provided by the teacher to better meet the criteria of a good question. Similarly, students can practice identifying appropriate sources, critique the evaluation of sources done by others, and reflect on whether or not a question has been sufficiently answered.

EXAMPLE: MIDDLE SCHOOL SCIENCE

An ex-student of mine who went on to teach middle school science told me that she designated every Friday as "media day" in her science classes. Her students brought in science-related articles from the newspaper or magazines, which allowed her to engage them in a discussion of scientific and information literacy.

Ask your students to find an article in a newspaper, magazine, or online that is making some type of scientific claim. Is the claim justified? Who is the source? How accurate and current is the information?

EXAMPLE: HIGH SCHOOL PHOTOGRAPHY

As you know, not everything is on the Internet. In fact, not everything one wants to know is to be found in electronic or print sources. Where else should students learn to look for useful information? Sometimes people themselves are a good and necessary source. But whom do I ask? What do I really want to know? Students can practice and improve their information literacy skills by figuring out whom and what to ask.

For example, in a photography class, students might be assigned to create a photomontage that captures some element of the spirit or heart of their town, county, or region. As research for the project, students must interview local inhabitants who can best help them get a sense of such an element. But whom should they interview? What should they ask? How will they know when they are "done"? Students can also be asked to reflect upon this information gathering as part of the assignment.

EXAMPLE: COLLEGE POLITICAL SCIENCE COURSE

Students might be asked to find and read a critique of a candidate's position on some issue. In addition to responding to the critique, students can be asked how they located the source. Also, students can be asked to evaluate the accuracy, relevancy, currency, and bias of the sources they considered as well as the one they finally settled upon. Such information literacy questions can be embedded in the larger assignment as part of a summative assessment so that the faculty are emphasizing and measuring information literacy skills alongside course-related ideas.

Or, such information literacy questions can be asked as standalone formative assessments to encourage their practice and provide opportunities for feedback and reflection on them. As with any skill, there needs to be frequent opportunities for practice of it. The more different settings where students see a skill employed, the more they will recognize its value as well.

Assessing Collaborative Skills

9

Along with the critical-thinking and information literacy skills mentioned in earlier chapters, employers are consistently asking for more and better collaborative skills from the workforce. Communities need individuals who can foster collaboration within and among the many organizations, committees, and institutions to function well. Families and relationships certainly benefit from healthy cooperation.

Furthermore, research has found that employing the structured cooperative activities in which students can learn collaborative skills also enhances their achievement, particularly when there are clear group goals and individual accountability (Ellis, 2001; Slavin, Hurley, & Chamberlain, 2003), and when students are taught skills that foster more effective group work (Slavin, 2006). Quite a bit of research has also found that working collaboratively fosters better intergroup relations, reducing prejudice and increasing acceptance of others (Myers, 2008).

Yet, we often do not directly teach skills such as collaboration. Too often we assume that if we just give learners enough group work, or enough research experience, or enough persuasive writing assignments they will inevitably become good collaborators, or information literate, or adept at argumentation. Too often that is not the case. Thus, if we value critical skills such as collaboration, we must explicitly teach and assess them.

COLLABORATIVE SKILLS

What do we mean by collaborative skills? Although a distinction is often made between collaborative learning and cooperative learning (Bruffee, 1995; Panitz, 1997), the terms collaborative skills and cooperative skills are often used interchangeably (e.g., Johnson & Johnson, 1994). The former will be adopted here.

Several frameworks of collaborative skills have been posited. For example, Johnson and Johnson (1991) identified three types of skills important to cooperative learning: 1) communication, 2) building and maintaining trust, and 3) controversy skills. Marzano et al. (1993) described and provided rubrics for the assessment of four collaborative skills: 1) "Works towards the achievement of group goals"; 2) "demonstrates effective interpersonal skills"; 3) "contributes to group maintenance"; and 4) "effectively performs a variety of goals within a group" (pp. 87-88). The model captured in the group performance rubric developed as part of the Connecticut Common Core of Learning (1989) also fleshes out collaborative skills in a detailed and effective manner. The rubric can be found in an article which describes the application of the rubric in a math setting (Collison, 1992) and online at <http://pals.sri.com/tasks/9-12/CarWash/rubric.html>.

As mentioned in Chapter 2, organizing a set of skills into such a framework or set of categories helps us better understand their relationship to each other and to the relevant context of group work. Working from the aforementioned frameworks and other group work rubrics, I have identified a set of categories that capture the critical collaborative skills.

Good collaborators should:

1) Participate in and contribute to group tasks
2) Stay focused on the task
3) Foster effective group functioning and relations
4) Communicate well

As with any such list of skills it is somewhat artificial to separate them as each one is quite dependent upon the others. "Communicate well" is probably the most redundant in that it is critical to each of the other skills. However, because effective communication is so critical in so many situations I have chosen to keep it as a separate category that can be targeted in instruction and assessment.

More specifically, and borrowing some language from the models previously discussed, the following represent some of the important skills under each category:

1) Participate in and contribute to group process
   • Accepts and fulfills role(s) within group
   • Performs fair share of work
   • Consistently and actively contributes knowledge, ideas, and skills
   • Asks questions and engages in discussion
   • Evaluates quality of own performance
   • Completes assignments outside of meetings
   • Persists despite obstacles
2) Stay focused on the task
   • Plans carefully before beginning work
   • Pays attention
   • Contributes to the establishment of group goals

- Follows agreed upon procedures
- Summarizes and asks clarifying questions to further progress
- Considers implications of actions
- Evaluates progress to determine if change is needed
- Guides group towards solution(s)
- Avoids disruptive behavior

3) Foster effective group functioning and relations
- Openly considers the ideas and perspectives of others
- Includes others by requesting input and asking questions
- Shares credit and blame
- Constructively provides and receives feedback
- Confronts, defines, and addresses conflict
- Guides group towards agreement, consensus, or compromise

4) Communicate well
- Expresses ideas clearly
- Speaks at appropriate volume and speed
- Listens respectively and objectively
- Balances listening and speaking well
- Gives eye contact and does not interrupt speaker
- Avoids tone or expression that suggests impatience, disgust, or sarcasm
- Accurately and clearly paraphrases or summarizes contributions of self and others

Although, as an educator, you might want to develop all of these skills, it is unrealistic to target all of them at once for instruction or assessment. Thus, I recommend identifying a small subset of these skills to assess and highlight in your classroom or media center. Continue to model and encourage the other skills as they go hand-in-hand with each other to promote effective collaboration, but specifically target a few. In Chapter 10, on the other hand, I will describe how a school or district might develop a more thorough and systematic scope and sequence for developing a set of skills.

SUMMATIVE ASSESSMENT

As you might imagine, summatively capturing a student's collaborative skills, even a subset of them, presents a unique challenge. To truly measure proficient application of these skills you would need to observe a student participating with others on a task in an authentic context. The logistics of assessing each student in such a group setting can be daunting. Moreover, it is unlikely a particular student would display the full range of collaborative skills in any given situation even if he has mastered them.

One solution would be to only assess collaborative skills at a group level. Instead of trying to find enough opportunities to assess each student on a variety of skills multiple times, simply assess how well the group as a whole is applying the skills. Fewer points of measurement would be required to get a good summative picture of collaborative skill achievement in your population.

However, if you want to assess collaborative skills for each student, consider the following process:

1) Select a subset of skills (perhaps 6 to10?) from the list on pages 92–93 (or your own list) to intentionally develop in your students.
2) Select 3 to 5 skills from the subset to more specifically target and assess.
3) Construct a series of pair or group assessment tasks to be completed near the end of the semester or year that target the smaller set of skills.
4) Plan backwards from your assessments to design instruction of these skills (see "formative assessment" on page 99).

To illustrate, imagine selecting eight skills from the list on pages 92–93:

- Accepts and fulfills role(s) within group
- Consistently and actively contributes knowledge, ideas, and skills
- Contributes to the establishment of group goals
- Summarizes and asks clarifying questions to further progress
- Openly considers the ideas and perspectives of others
- Includes others by requesting input and asking questions
- Balances listening and speaking well
- Gives eye contact and does not interrupt speaker

Of those eight skills, you could expressly target the following four skills:

- Contributes to the establishment of group goals
- Summarizes and asks clarifying questions to further progress
- Openly considers the ideas and perspectives of others
- Includes others by requesting input and asking questions

Next, construct a series of tasks through which you could assess the four skills. Remember, collaboration takes quite a variety of forms in school and outside of it. For example, opportunities for collaboration can occur in formal group projects, committee meetings, online discussions, peer review or editing, tutoring, group problem solving, and one-on-one informal conversations among others. So, you would like to provide a variety of settings in which students could apply the skills. Observing the behavior in multiple and varied situations will also increase the validity of inferences drawn.

Thus, select a few different forms of collaboration. Borrowing from the assessment types used for information literacy in Chapter 8, assessment of the application of collaborative skills in these settings could take the form of scenarios, logs or journals, or direction observation. Additionally, a teacher or librarian cannot always be present when collaboration is occurring. So, you can also utilize a variety of means of collecting evidence including self, peer, and other assessment.

EXAMPLE: HIGH SCHOOL SOCIAL STUDIES

For example, in a semester-long high school social studies course, after developing the collaborative skills for the first three months, I could assess these skills over the last month. Specifically, my assessment mix could include a scenario such as the following, perhaps as homework.

Group Collaboration Constructed-Response Task

Read the following scenario of a group working on a research project. Analyze how effectively the group collaborated on the task by answering the questions that follow the scenario.

Scenario

Rachel: *I don't know what we are supposed to be doing.*

Devin: *Me either.*

Charyce: *Well, let's see what the assignment says. She says here that we have to come up with a list of reasons why Pilgrims came to America. Then we are supposed to compare that with why Mexicans are coming to this country now to see if it is similar or not. Then we have to present it to the class.*

Devin: *But does she mention how we are supposed to do our presentation?*

Jaclyn: *What do you mean, how we do it?*

Devin: *I mean, do we write a paper, or just stand up and explain what we did, or make a poster, or like we did last year in Mr. Johnson's class, we could do like a radio show.*

Rachel: *Yeah, let's do a radio show. I could be the sportscaster.*

Jaclyn: *Well, we've got four days to do this, counting today. Why don't we divide up the jobs?*

Rachel: *But how are we supposed to get all this done?*

Charyce: *Maybe Devin's right. If we figure out what kind of presentation we want to do, we can figure out better how to do the other parts.*

Jaclyn: *I think we should decide who's doing what.*

Rachel: *I already said, I'll be the sportscaster.*

Charyce: *And what are you going to talk about?*

Rachel: *I don't know.*

Charyce: *Exactly. Let's figure out what kind of presentation first.*

Jaclyn: *But who's going to do the research on this stuff?*

continued on next page

Devin: *Well, Jaclyn, if we know what kind of presentation we're going to do, then wouldn't we be more likely to know what part of the work we'd do?*
Charyce: *Yeah, so let's do a newscast, and Rachel can be a sportscaster.*
Rachel: *Awesome!*
Charyce: *Okay, so, Jaclyn, if we are dividing up the work like you suggested, what job would you like?*
Jaclyn: *I'll research the Pilgrims.*
Devin: *I guess I'll research the Mexicans.*
Charyce: *And I'll help both of you with the research, and Rachel can organize the newscast.*
Rachel: *What, the* whole *thing?*
Devin, Charyce, Jaclyn: *Yes!*

Questions, *tied to the four skills,* might include:
1) What goal or goals did the group establish? Which member most actively contributed to the establishment of the group goal(s)? Briefly explain.
2) Which member least contributed to the establishment of the group goal(s)? Briefly explain.
3) Identify two places in the group dialogue where a member summarized or asked a clarifying question to further progress in the group.
4) Did member X openly consider the ideas and perspectives of others? Identify evidence to support your position.
5) Identify a point in the dialogue where you think it would have been helpful to summarize or ask a clarifying question. What would you have said?

A rubric to assess the answers on such a constructed-response assessment might look like the example in Figure 9.1.

Figure 9.1: Rubric for Analyzing Group Collaboration

Group Collaboration Scenario Rubric			
Analyzed scenario regarding members'...			
Contributing to establishment of goals	Insufficiently	Adequately	Accurately and Clearly
Summarizing and asking clarifying questions	Insufficiently	Adequately	Accurately and Clearly
Openly considering others' ideas and perspectives	Insufficiently	Adequately	Accurately and Clearly
Including others in group process	Not addressed on this task		

Obviously, the scenario task only reveals students' *understanding* of when and how to apply the skills. To also gather some evidence of their own application of the skills, you could ask students to keep a journal across the semester in which they reflect upon their application and their group or pair's application of the four collaborative skills being targeted. These would be brief entries in which they respond to one or two prompts such as:

- Give two examples of times you contributed to the establishment of group goals.
- In the just completed peer editing task, did you ever encourage your partner to participate more by requesting input, asking questions, or some other means? Explain. Did your partner ever encourage you to participate more by requesting input, asking questions, or some other means? Explain. As we have done in the past, you will have a chance to discuss yours and your partner's answers with each other.
- If someone were to ask you if you openly considered the ideas and perspectives of others in our large class discussions this semester, how would you answer that person?
- Select two of the four collaborative skills we focused on this semester. Describe the progress you have made in the development of those two skills. Use examples to support your points.

A rubric to assess such journal responses could look like the example in Figure 9.2.

Figure 9.2: Rubric for Journal Entries

Journal Entry Rubric			
Answered the question asked	Little or no alignment between question and answer	Answer relates to, but not completely in line with, question	Answer directly addresses the question
Thoroughly addressed question	Minimal answer— little or no detail provided	Some detail but more needed to fully answer question	Sufficient detail provided to answer question
Provided specific examples when called for	Appropriate examples are not provided	Some examples but not completely appropriate or sufficient	Appropriate and sufficient examples provided

Finally, to acquire more direct evidence of the students' collaborative skills you could observe groups of students engaged in a structured task in which the group members are teaching each other about specific concepts with a goal of leading a class discussion on the topic. By embedding this assessment into your instruction, you have not had to create an assessment of collaborative skills that takes time away from student learning. You could facilitate student engagement in meaningful social construction of understanding while also observing the application of the targeted skills.

You could modify the Group Collaboration Scenario Rubric just slightly to apply to your assessment of the students' collaboration skills in the structured learning task. You would probably add a notes column to the rubric so, if desired, you could provide a little more detailed feedback. In addition to your observations of their skills in these groups, you could also include a peer and self-assessment of these skills in your assessment package.

EXAMPLE: SECOND GRADE CLASSROOM

The same set of four collaborative skills could be targeted in a second grade classroom, just at a less sophisticated level. For example, *asking clarifying questions to further progress* at the high school level might include "If we do decide to give a *video* presentation, how will we use the class time available to work on it?" Whereas, at the second grade level, it might sound like "What do you mean by 'borrowing ten'?" or "How did you get that ten there?"

To assess the second graders' application of the targeted skills near the end of the year, you could again observe their group performance in a variety of settings much as you would with older students. However, second graders are not quite ready to respond to a scenario like the high school example. Instead, you might show the class a brief clip of a movie in which animated characters or real people collaborate on some task. Then pose a question to the class such as "Did any character try to encourage members of the group to participate or help out the group? How did the character encourage the other group members?" Then, show the clip a second time asking the class to specifically look for an answer to those two questions. After showing the clip a second time, ask each student to write down the name of one character that encouraged others to join in, and to describe what the character did or said to do so.

In lieu of a journal, I might ask my second graders to complete an occasional self-assessment on one or more of the collaborative skills.

Collaborative Self-Assessment Question
When you worked with your partner on the tall tale book, did you listen carefully and consider your partner's ideas? Circle one:
Not very much   Some of the time   Most of the time
Did your partner listen carefully and consider your ideas? Circle one:
Not very much   Some of the time   Most of the time

You would also want to observe the students in pair and group settings as they worked on a variety of tasks and record their performance on a simple rubric. In other words, to summatively assess the targeted skills, you would collect multiple and varied evidence of students' understanding and application of these critical skills. Although you would be teaching a variety of collaborative skills, you would likely be satisfied if your students demonstrated growth (as second graders) or proficiency (as high school students) on the four skills targeted. They would be much better collaborators as a result.

FORMATIVE ASSESSMENT

To acquire such complex interpersonal skills takes considerable time and effort. Thus, to prepare students to perform well on substantial summative assessments of the skills will require careful and systematic development of the skills. That means once again following the four steps of skill building I outlined earlier: 1) instruction and modeling, 2) practice, 3) feedback, and 4) reflection.

INSTRUCTION AND MODELING

If a skill is to be acquired the learner should be cognizant of the skill. That is, the learner should understand what behaviors are representative of the skill and what it looks like when performed well. Thus, the first step in developing collaborative skills is to expressly describe and display them for your students. This can happen in various ways. You could simply name and describe the set of six to ten skills you intend to focus on and the three to five skills you will emphasize the most.

Or, you could begin with a discussion amongst your students initiated through a viewing of examples of good and bad collaboration in film or on TV. Have students identify what was effective or not effective. Perhaps lead them in the process of creating a list of such skills. You might choose from among that list or guide them to some predetermined set, or some combination of the two.

Whichever path you take to identifying a small set of skills, follow that up with modeling and examples. You want everyone to be clear of the nature and value of the skills you are targeting. Of course, modeling will continue throughout your class or sessions as you highlight, and have students highlight, particular examples of the skills as they occur. "Did anyone in the group notice how Sarah guided your group back towards the goal? How did she do that?"

PRACTICE

The most effective instruction of the skills will be in the course of the students' practice of them as the students will eventually construct their own meaning of effective application of the skills. Give them multiple opportunities to apply the skills in a variety of contexts. As mentioned before, this does not mean each opportunity for practice must involve an elaborate and authentic task.

Rather, it is quite useful to occasionally isolate a specific skill by giving students brief situations in which you explicitly target one (or occasionally two) skills so students can focus their practice on that distinct skill. This will also permit more precise formative assessment of the skills since you can observe progress on each one.

For example, give your middle school students a brief role-playing situation. Before they begin conducting individual research in the media center, have them pair up and pretend for the moment that they will be collaborating on the research task. Ask them to identify one or two goals they could accomplish by the end of the day's session.

Once again, do not just give students this brief exercise and assume the learning you have in mind will take place. Make explicit that the purpose of the exercise is to practice one of the targeted skills: *Contributes to the establishment of group goals*. Take another minute to ask individuals from a few pairs how their partners helped them identify a realistic goal.

In addition to some smaller, targeted practice, a more elaborate task could be a group project in which each group would create a video of an imaginary team working on some task. Each video would contain examples of effective and ineffective demonstration of the targeted skills. Discussing and planning the video would further enhance the students' understanding of the targeted skills. You could then use some of the better videos in subsequent classes.

FEEDBACK

Feedback on the students' practice of collaborative skills can take multiple forms as well. For example, as described on page 96, ask students to keep "collaborative journals" in which they describe the progress they are making in developing the targeted skills or responding to prompts. You can then provide occasional and limited feedback to their journal entries. Remember, good feedback (Sadler, 1989):

1) identifies the standard or reference that is targeted, in this case the skill
2) identifies the discrepancy between performance and the standard
3) suggests action to address the gap between the two

Fortunately, the practice of collaboration requires students to interact with each other. That means peers can provide an additional and effective source of feedback. Encourage your students to do so on their own in a constructive manner. However, you can also design specific means for peers to provide such feedback. They can complete anonymous assessments, engage in group postmortems, or provide whole-class critiques of group role-play exercises, to name a few.

Again, construct such peer feedback opportunities so they explicitly target the specific skills and so students provide feedback that is consistent with the characteristics of good feedback. As I am sure you have already recognized, *constructively providing and receiving feedback* is another valuable collaborative skill that will require some modeling and practice.

REFLECTION

Many of the opportunities for practice and feedback previously described serve as good vehicles for reflection as well. If certain discrepancies between performance of the skill and the standard have been identified, ignoring or glossing over them will not help. Students need to examine their strengths and weaknesses if they are to best take advantage of the feedback. "What can I most improve upon? Why do I think I perform that skill well? Why am I good at that in one situation but not in another? What have I learned I need to do to get better at that skill? I think I am good team player, so why do I have so many conflicts with other group members?"

Obviously, reflection of this sort can occur in reflection or collaboration journals. For example, to address a specific discrepancy, students could identify a goal to improve a particular skill. Students could assess their progress or growth on that skill over time in the journal.

If you use peer or other feedback, students should be given some opportunity to reflect on it as well. The more regular such feedback is, the easier it will be for students to accept and digest, and the better they will become at reflecting upon it. Such reflection can even take place orally within the group itself. At the end of a collaboration, ask the partners or group members to review their expression of one or more of the targeted skills. "Did members balance their listening and speaking? Did we avoid disruptive behavior? What could we do better next time in terms of contributing ideas and skills or confronting and addressing conflict?"

As I have mentioned repeatedly, it is critical to explicitly identify the skills you are targeting in the modeling, practice, feedback, and reflection of them; in particular, the small set of skills you are assessing. However, just because you are assessing a few skills do not ignore the other collaborative skills. The smaller subset does not occur in isolation. So, feel free to regularly comment upon or identify or ask questions about some of the other skills. Students should learn the targeted set better if placed in a more complex, authentic context that includes all the skills.

Some of the suggestions in this chapter, as in previous chapters, would require the trading off of teaching something else to foster these collaborative skills. That is a decision educators contemplate regularly. However, if you are concerned about losing some of the content of your course, I would just ask you to consider again the question that runs through this book: What content are you going to teach that is *more* valuable than the development of these skills . . . for school, work, or life?

If you answer that question with an eagerness to jump in with both feet or just a willingness to stick your toe into the pool, the last two chapters are designed for you. In Chapter 10, we will explore how the development and assessment of critical skills can be systematically developed across a school or district's curriculum. Good skill development will require an ongoing assessment effort building on prior instruction, practice, feedback, and reflection.

However, if this is fairly new to you, you are still a bit unsure of its value, you are not sure if there would be much school-wide support for such efforts,

Assessing Skills at the School and District Level   10

For students to become truly proficient at these skills, it will require considerable practice across grades, systematically building these skills from year to year. Unfortunately, not only are these critical skills receiving insufficient attention in school, the attention they do receive is haphazard and inconsistent. If these skills are to be fully developed, an entire school or district needs to design a plan that intentionally and systematically guides their development.

How would a school or district begin to design such a plan for the assessment of a critical skill, say, information literacy? In the authentic assessment model, assessment drives the curriculum. Thus, I would recommend a school or district first create an exit assessment for its oldest students by following the four steps described in Chapter 5. Information literacy skills can be learned at a very young age, so I am going to illustrate this approach by developing a sample plan for teaching and assessing information literacy skills for an elementary school. However, the approach described below certainly could be applied to the development of *any* skill at *any* level.

STEP 1: IDENTIFY THE STANDARDS

Specifically, a K-5 school (or all such schools in a district) could create an exit assessment for its fifth graders. Step 1 in such a process is to identify the standards for the subject matter. For information literacy, the five standards listed in Chapter 8 were:

- Define or frame a question to be answered
- Locate appropriate sources of information that address the question
- Access information from a variety of electronic and non-electronic sources
- Evaluate the accuracy, relevancy, authority, and currency of the information for the question
- Determine when sufficient information has been acquired to answer the question

Is it realistic to expect fifth graders to be capable of these skills at a fairly sophisticated level? Yes, if beginning in kindergarten these students have been given many opportunities to practice and reflect upon the skills; if the skills have been integrated throughout the curriculum; if the skills have been regularly assessed with frequent feedback provided to staff and students. If a school decided these skills were important enough, the school could make it happen.

Once a set of exit standards was identified, the standards could be scaled down to third- and first-grade benchmark standards. Benchmark standards describe progress along the way toward a final set of standards. All teachers, library media specialists, and other staff working with kindergartners and first graders would have a clear set of goals to guide their instruction. Similarly, second and third grade staff would target the third-grade standards. Finally, all staff would keep an eye on the exit standards that fifth graders would be expected to meet.

If the above skills describe the fifth-grade or exit standards, what might the first- and third-grade benchmark standards look like?

STATE STANDARDS OF INFORMATION LITERACY

A few states have fleshed out standards for information literacy along specific benchmarks. For example, Kansas has clearly and effectively spelled out standards and benchmarks for *every* grade from pre-K through twelfth grade. Instructional examples are also provided for each benchmark. The State of Wisconsin standards for Information and Inquiry delineate benchmarks for the end of fourth, eighth, and twelfth grade. Montana also uses fourth, eighth, and twelfth grades as benchmarks.

Utah provides "objectives" of Library Media for grades 3, 4, 5, 6, and 7-12. As part of its Essential Knowledge and Skills for Technology Applications, the State of Texas identifies "information acquisition" skills for grades K-2, 3-5, and 6-8. One of Tennessee's six standards for computer technology addresses my more narrow definition of information literacy. Benchmarks are identified at every grade level from K through eighth, with a final benchmark for students in grades 9-12. See the information literacy standards and benchmarks from Oklahoma, New Jersey, and Nevada for other examples. You can find links to all these state standards at <http://edstandards.org/StSu/InfoLit.html>.

Given the fifth-grade exit standards listed in Step 1: Identify the Standards, and borrowing language from some of the state standards in the State Standards of Information Literacy section, third-grade benchmarks might include:

Third Grade Benchmarks— Information Literacy

Defining Question: Develop a focused question related to a topic

- Define a question that addresses topic with limited assistance
- Identify subtopics and formulate a variety of questions related to them (Utah)
- Refine question as information need changes (Kansas)

Locating Sources: Locate information relevant to question

- Determine types of information needed to answer question
- Locate and utilize a variety of information sources and formats found in school
- Efficiently use the library media center's classification system to locate resources
- Evaluate and select possible sources based on currency, genre, and relevance to topic (Wisconsin)

Accessing Information: Access information from a variety of familiar resources

- Acquire information in a variety of formats (e.g., text, images, video)
- Access information from most features (e.g., charts/tables, headings/ subheadings, index) of print resources
- With some guidance, apply appropriate electronic search strategies including keyword and Boolean
- With limited prompting, use online help and seek human assistance
- Construct a bibliography with full citation (Kansas)

Evaluating Information: Evaluate and select information that is accurate, relevant, current, and authoritative

- Seek multiple sources to verify accuracy of information (Kansas)
- Select information relevant to question
- Identify the sponsoring organization or author for all resources (Wisconsin)
- Determine timeliness of information sources (Wisconsin)
- With guidance, recognize how facts, opinions, and points of view differ from one another (Kansas)

Answered Question: Identify criteria for judging completeness of answer to question

- With guidance, determine if information acquired sufficiently answers question
- Determine if teacher/media specialist-provided criteria have been met

Scaling down those standards further, first-grade benchmarks might include:

First Grade Benchmarks— Information Literacy

Defining Question: Identify an information need

- Recognize a need for information
- Formulate broad questions with limited prompting (Kansas)
- Can respond to a broad question with a more specific question of his/her own (Kansas)

Locating Sources: Identify a variety of potential sources of information (Kansas)

- Identify and distinguish between different types of information (e.g., fiction/nonfiction) found in different types of sources
- Identify people who are possible information sources (Utah)
- With guidance, recognize type of information relevant to a question
- Use initial information (e.g., title, table of contents, pictures) to determine appropriateness of source
- Utilize the library media center's sections (e.g., fiction vs. nonfiction reference) to locate sources
- Select more than one resource or format when appropriate
- Select information resources that are understandable and available (Utah)

Accessing information: Access basic information from a few sources

- Acquire information in more than one format (e.g., text and images)
- Access information from basic features (e.g., table of contents, text, pictures) of print sources
- With supervision, perform simple search of electronic sources to acquire information (Tennessee)
- Construct a simple bibliography with author/title (Kansas)

Evaluating Information: Recognize information that is relevant and current

- Distinguish between examples of accurate and inaccurate information
- Distinguish between relevant and irrelevant information in a source
- With guidance, identify indicators of timeliness of information in a source
- With guidance, identify facts and opinions in information sources

Answered Question: Distinguish between complete and very incomplete answers to questions

- Recognize a need for additional information
- Recognize more than one indicator that a question has not been fully answered

Note: If you would like to flesh out benchmarks in even more detail, I would recommend you look at the Kansas and Utah standards at the link on page 104.

STEP 2: CREATE AN AUTHENTIC TASK

Once the standards are identified, the next step is to develop measures through which students can demonstrate they have met the standards. However, it is not necessary to measure every student's performance. A school or district could create an assessment simply to provide school- or district-wide feedback. To that end, an assessment of information literacy could be administered to a random sample of 30 fifth graders (out of a class of 100) near the end of the school year. Those scores could provide ample evidence of how well students in that school are meeting the exit standards and provide meaningful information about what skills were acquired and which were not.

Of course, to get meaningful information from such a sample you will want to ensure it is randomly selected. Using some other means of selecting your sample, such as teacher recommendations, could, for example, skew the sample to more favored or more proficient students. Additionally, if your student population is large enough, and you are interested in how certain subgroups perform on the assessment, you could apply stratified random sampling. In this method you would select randomly from each subgroup and combine the subgroup samples for the total sample. Normally, you would select the same proportion (e.g., 30%) from each subgroup to create a proportionately stratified random sample. (See Fink, 2002, for more discussion on selecting a good sample.)

To make the exit assessment process manageable and meaningful, I would suggest a blended assessment that includes some forced-choice items and some performance-based or authentic tasks. The random sample of fifth graders, in groups, could be brought down to the media center to complete a 45- to 60-minute assessment near the end of fifth grade.

What might such an assessment look like? It could include 8 to 10 multiple-choice questions that address knowledge and comprehension of relevant terminology or skills. Additionally, students could be given several tasks in the media center in which they must demonstrate that they can locate appropriate sources, access relevant information from electronic and non-electronic sources, evaluate the information and sources, and, finally, determine if the information need or question has been answered. If a somewhat larger sample of students was tested, the length of the assessment could be reduced by randomly assigning a subset (e.g., six of eight) of the performance tasks to each student. Across all the students each question would be administered a sufficient number of times.

For example, a task like the one in Chapter 8 on *Defining a Question* could be included:

Task
Imagine that you are interested in nutrition and vitamins. Write a specific question you could research that is related to that topic.
OR

Task
Imagine that you are interested in the general topic of nutrition and vitamins. Circle the questions below that represent a narrower or more specific topic related to the general topic. • What is a healthy lifestyle? • How does the human body use vitamins? • How many minutes a day should someone your age exercise? • Can too many vitamins be harmful?

To assess the fifth graders' ability to access information, a task similar to the one described in Chapter 8 could be used:

Task
Identify which keywords and Boolean operators you might use to search for the topics below. (Or, have students search for some specific topics.)

To assess the fifth graders' ability to evaluate information, a task similar to one described in Chapter 8 could be used:

Task
Imagine you were investigating the question. . . . In the course of your research you visited a Web site (or found a book) entitled " " which described. . . . Describe **how** you would check the accuracy, relevancy, authority, and currency of the site (or book) **for your question.**

Or, for a more hands-on task, you could send students to two Web sites (or other sources) and ask them to evaluate the sites for a particular question. The students' evaluations could take the form of a brief written response to questions of accuracy, currency, authority, and relevancy, or you could interview each student in real-time as they review the sites.

STEP 3: IDENTIFY THE CRITERIA

What does it look like when a fifth-grade student has effectively located appropriate sources or evaluated the information in terms of the question being investigated? To be able to draw valid inferences regarding performance on such tasks, the characteristics of good performance on the tasks, the criteria, should be identified.

For example, for the *Defining a Question* task described on page 106, the criteria would be "narrows topic" and "question is within scope of original topic." Criteria would be identified for each of the performance tasks on the exit assessment.

STEP 4: CREATE A RUBRIC

The multiple-choice items on the exit assessment would be scored as usual. However, scoring the student performance on the authentic tasks requires more subjective judgment from the evaluators. Thus, authentic tasks often include rubrics which can lead to more consistent scoring of students.

As described in Chapter 5, creating a rubric begins with the criteria. If there are more than a couple of criteria for a task, an analytic rubric, which measures performance on each criterion independently, is preferable. For example, to continue with the criteria listed in Step 3, see a simple analytic rubric illustrated in Figure 10.1.

Figure 10.1: Rubric for Framing a Research Question

Framing a Research Question Rubric			
Criteria	**Limited**	**Adequate**	**Proficient**
Narrows topic	Research question remains vague or excessively broad or narrow	Research question has been narrowed to a fairly decipherable and manageable topic	Research question is appropriately specific and coherently defined
Question within scope of original topic	Research question primarily falls outside of original topic	Although the research question does not lie completely within original topic, it is sufficiently related	Research question clearly falls within general scope

Finally, scoring the assessment would involve assigning points for the correct forced-choice items and applying rubrics to the performance tasks. The data would then be used to measure the progress and performance of the exiting fifth graders and to provide feedback to the staff of the school on which skills need to be better addressed. Even administering the assessment every two years should provide valuable information.

WHAT ABOUT THE EARLIER GRADES?

The fifth-grade exit assessment in this example could be a school's only formal assessment of information literacy. Even just randomly sampling 30 fifth graders should give a school a good picture of how well its students are meeting the standards. However, other formal assessments, at first and third grade for example, could be administered, which would be particularly helpful if there were significant student turnover at the school. Regardless, frequent and systematic *formative* assessment should be a regular part of the school's program if information literacy is a critical goal.

FORMATIVE ASSESSMENT

That means, beginning in kindergarten, students should be asked on a regular basis to identify an information need or define a research question; locate a variety of sources relevant to the question; access useful information from those sources; evaluate the information retrieved; and learn to judge when a question has been sufficiently answered. Most of this practice, particularly at a younger age, would target individual skills such as locating a source or considering if additional information is needed. A clever example of a simple formative task for a younger child can be found among the Kansas instructional examples. Students create two birthday invitations, one with accurate information (e.g., date, location) and one with inaccurate information, to learn to distinguish between the two when evaluating sources.

Furthermore, the practice that kindergartners receive should be aligned with what follows in first grade so that skill acquisition builds upon prior learning in a systematic manner. Aligning standards across the grades is only the first step. Conversations around the alignment of instruction and formative assessment across grade levels must also occur if you want to unleash the potential of this process.

Certain of these informal checks should be identified as data gathering checkpoints through which educators can monitor the progress of the kindergartners and first graders as they move toward the first-grade benchmarks, the progress of second and third graders toward the third- grade benchmarks, and the progress of the fourth and fifth graders toward the exit standards. It does not need to be cumbersome. A few pieces of data gathered a few times will provide sufficient feedback to students, teachers, and library media specialists about the current strengths and deficiencies of students' information literacy skills. That information, in turn, can be used to adjust instruction and learning.

FINAL THOUGHTS

Yes, this takes a school-wide effort and some time. That is why it is advisable for a school or district to only attempt to assess one or two of these critical skills in such a systematic manner, at least to begin with. Also, this is just one approach for developing a school- or district-wide plan. (See Fisher et al. (2007/2008) for another model used at the high school level.) Yet, if a school chooses to follow such a plan, including the design of systematic instruction and formative assessment of the skills, the results would likely be remarkable. In fact, post the standards and benchmarks, the exit assessment (or a facsimile thereof), and a summary of student performance on the school's or district's Web site. Parents and community members, I believe, would be quite impressed with the level of their fifth graders' information literacy skills.

Starting Small (Meaningful and Manageable) 11

I am acutely aware of the workload of teachers and library media specialists in our schools. So, when Mueller says, "Here's one more thing you should be doing in your classrooms or media centers," I understand if your first response is to cringe. However, first, I hope the message delivered in the previous chapters has persuaded you that teaching and assessing these skills is critical. Second, I hope to illustrate in this chapter how you can begin this valuable process in a small and manageable manner.

By starting small I mean:

- Identify just a small subset of skills within the domain you are targeting
- Deliberately provide a little instruction and modeling of the skills
- Provide a few opportunities for practice of the skills spaced throughout your semester or year
- Formatively assess the skills and provide feedback embedded in your instruction and practice
- Summatively assess the skills in a simple manner
- Collaborate with your fellow teachers and librarians on the above steps where possible

To illustrate, I will describe one path a classroom teacher could take to begin implementing the assessment of a critical skill. Then, I will describe a path a library media specialist could follow to similarly encourage the growth of such a skill.

THE CLASSROOM TEACHER
SELF-ASSESSMENT SKILLS

As critical as it is that we assess students on the skills described in the text, I believe it is even more important that students learn to assess themselves on these skills. Students are often too dependent on others for judgment. "Is this good?" "Am I done?" "Do you think I have found enough information?" As adults, we have to make many of these decisions ourselves. Few of our students are very capable of it. Thus, one of the most critical skills our students can develop is the ability of self-assessment.

So, we will consider the skill of self-assessment to illustrate how a classroom teacher can begin to assess a skill that is not typically part of her evaluation mix. Alternatively, you could pick a skill that you would like to develop and imagine how you could implement this process for that skill.

As described in Chapter 2, someone can be considered proficient in self-assessment if he can apply relevant criteria to his own work, identify strengths and weaknesses in his work or process, and judge when said work is completed. Additionally, reflective self-assessment includes goal-setting skills such as the ability to identify clear and realistic goals, identify goals relevant to the task, and identify effective responses to positive and negative outcomes.

Identify Small Subset of Skills

Start small; do not try to tackle all of those skills at once. Perhaps focus on the first two: 1) can apply relevant criteria to own work, and 2) can identify strengths and weaknesses in work or process. Those two skills tie together nicely and are very valuable skills on their own.

Provide Instruction and Modeling of the Skills

It is likely that you already teach your students to apply relevant criteria and identify strengths and weaknesses to some degree. The only difference here is that you will deliberately identify these skills to your students as skills you intend to focus on in your classroom. Thus, you will look for particular opportunities in your instruction to highlight where these skills can be applied. Then, you would model how the skills can be applied in those contexts.

One good tool at your disposal for such instruction is the rubric. If you have created rubrics to guide the development and assessment of certain student work, you can illustrate how the rubric can be used to *apply relevant criteria to own work*. For example, if you assign a research paper, apply the criteria in your research paper rubric to a sample paper. Show students how you would evaluate the paper in terms of the criteria. Teachers often collect old samples of student work for this purpose. However, do not just give students opportunities to apply the rubric. You need to deliberately talk about and distinguish between good and poor application of criteria. I have seen people go out and play tennis repeatedly with very little improvement. If we have not learned what to focus on when we practice a skill it is difficult to know how to improve it.

As another example of modeling, I talk to my Educational Psychology students about how I know if I have a good test. First, I will ask them what they think makes a good test. Then, I will take the list they have generated and explain how I apply those criteria to my tests. Are there a sufficient number of questions? Do the questions address a representative sample of the domain being tested? Are the items pitched at an appropriate level? And so on. My students are able to observe (hopefully) expert thought in process.

Intentionally find other places in your instruction to talk about what constitutes strengths and weaknesses on a task. Ask your students why it is important to identify both. Which do you often prefer to hear about? Which might be more useful to learn about? What can I do with that information?

Finally, it bears repeating that trading class time to more intentionally develop these skills can provide significant benefits in the long run. With students carefully reflecting on the strengths and weaknesses of their work, and learning to value that self-evaluation and self-improvement, they should produce better work and construct a deeper understanding of what you are teaching.

Provide Opportunities for Practice

Similarly, I would argue it would be worthwhile to turn over some class time to the practice of these skills. Some of the practice can be in the context of the ongoing work you assign, and some can be standalone practice of these skills. For example, to promote practice applying the skill of *apply relevant criteria to own work*, you can ask students to complete one or more of the following brief tasks:

- Take a few minutes to apply a rubric to their current work
- With a partner, apply a rubric to each other's work
- Apply just a *single* criterion to a sample of their own or other's work
- In class or as a brief homework assignment, write a brief reflection on how well their work matches the criteria
- Critique a sample of work along the criteria provided
- Answer one or two multiple choice questions that ask them to apply relevant criteria or evaluate if criteria have been applied appropriately
- Discuss what the criteria for judging performance on a task should be

To promote practice applying the skill of *identify strengths and weaknesses in work or process*, you can ask students to do many of the same brief tasks including:

- Take a few moments to identify strengths and weaknesses in a piece of their work
- Identify strengths and weaknesses in *how* (process) they do something
- Identify a *single* strength or weakness
- Identify and reflect upon a strength or weakness in their work, explaining why they have identified it as such

- Identify strengths and weaknesses in a work other than their own, another student's or a mock sample
- Explain why something is a strength or weakness in terms of the relevant criteria
- Answer one or two multiple choice questions that ask them to identify a strength or weakness in a sample of work or analyze if an imaginary other accurately identified the strengths or weaknesses in a sample
- Provide feedback to their peers in pairs, small groups, or to the whole class

Formatively Assess the Skills and Provide Feedback

Each of the above tasks could serve as a formative assessment as well. That is, in addition to the practice the task provides, it can also be used to convey information to you and your students about their progress on the development of the skill. That information, in turn, can be used to further refine their practice and your instruction. So, for a few practice tasks, collect students' answers or reflection to assess their progress.

To ensure sufficient effort on these tasks, particularly homework assignments, you might want to grade some of their work. However, that does not need to be a significant burden either. I adapted a grading scheme I learned from Barbara Walvoord at the University of Notre Dame. I assign a number of very brief assignments (each requiring just a few sentences) in which students must respond to the assigned readings or practice a skill. I give each of their responses a (+) or a (-). A (+) means the student put in a "good faith effort" on the task. In other words, I do not grade it on accuracy. If a student receives 90% pluses on the assignments she receives an A for the tasks. 80% pluses earns the student a B. And so on. I write few if any comments on the assignments. Consequently, it only takes me five to ten minutes to assign grades to a stack of 30 such papers.

With many of the assignments, I also take class time to briefly review them to provide feedback and to encourage their peers to provide feedback. I occasionally ask questions that encourages reflection on the feedback.

Of course, formative assessment can also include informal checks that are not collected or graded. Through class discussion of task responses or just walking around during their practice you can assess the progress being made, and you can provide feedback informally.

How often should you assign such tasks in class or for homework? To start small, if you took a few minutes once a week to overtly model and encourage practice of these skills, that would be sufficient to foster some significant growth in your students' self-assessment abilities, and in their disposition to assessing themselves in other contexts.

Summatively Assess the Skills

Finally, if you want to seriously foster your students' progress on these skills, you should also get a final check of proficiency at self-assessment. There are a variety of ways to collect such data in a single summative measure. For example, you could add a component to a significant assignment your students are completing near the end of the semester or year. That component could ask them to analyze a draft of their work (or the completed work) in terms of the relevant criteria. For a summative assessment, you may no longer point them to the specific criteria they should apply, but see if they can identify *and* apply them.

Or give students a separate task in which they must analyze a provided sample of work in terms of the criteria, or in terms of its strengths and weaknesses, or both. The burden of adding one more task (or, preferably, replacing another assignment with this one) should be outweighed by your students' gains.

This final assessment can also serve to guide your plans for instruction, modeling, practice, and feedback as you work towards promoting good performance on the summative assessment. Once you have a good sense of where you want your students to end up, you can target your instruction more clearly to that end. In authentic assessment, it is okay to teach to the test.

To recap, one path to begin assessing a critical skill would be:

- Select a skill that you really value but that you are not deliberately assessing in your class
- Choose one or two subskills within that broader skill to emphasize
- Design a summative assessment of one or more of the subskills
- Intentionally model and describe the subskills on a regular (but not necessarily frequent) basis
- Provide varied and regular (but not necessarily frequent) opportunities for students to practice the subskills
- Provide feedback through formative assessment of their practice
- Summatively assess in a simple yet meaningful manner to give yourself a good sense of how well the subskills were developed

Finally, any or all of the steps can be made even easier or more productive if done in collaboration with one or more of your school colleagues. For example, you will find that many librarians are fluent in a number of the critical skills you seek to develop such as information literacy and problem solving. Moreover, you will often find eagerness in your library staff to partner with you to find meaningful ways to integrate critical skills with the content you are teaching to create authentic assignments and assessments.

In other words, you could collaborate on the first two steps to agree upon a subskill or two on which to focus. Then draw upon the unique expertise you each bring to develop tasks appropriate for developing those subskills. Extend instruction and practice of those subskills beyond your classroom to the library media center or other settings conducive to their development. The more varied contexts in which your students practice and reflect upon these skills the more likely they will transfer them to other meaningful situations. As Harada and Yoshina (2005) state, "The point is that the instructors work as a team to make the learning experience a dynamic and seamless one for the students" (p. 12).

THE LIBRARY MEDIA SPECIALIST

For the library media specialist, who does not usually have such curricular control over students' learning, fostering a critical skill in a small yet systematic manner is not so easy. In the best case, you work in a school that values and even seeks out your expertise and participation in the design and delivery of the curriculum. In such a case you can collaborate with a teacher or a team or a department on the following process. If, on the other hand, you are not intentionally welcomed into the curriculum design and delivery process at your school, implementing even a small plan for developing a critical skill may require some "stealth assessment."

PROBLEM-SOLVING SKILLS

Let's start with the more collaborative setting, and then I will follow with a few suggestions for those requiring a more stealth approach. To illustrate one way a library media specialist can lead or collaborate in efforts to develop and assess a critical skill, beginning on a small scale, I will focus on a skill that is well aligned with your strengths—problem solving.

Librarians and media specialists recognize how the problem-solving process closely parallels the steps of finding useful information. Both begin with defining the question or problem to be answered or solved. Then, the parameters of the task need to be explored by considering and locating appropriate sources or relevant features of the problem. Once the task is more clearly set, relevant information can be accessed and possible solutions can be considered. Those solutions and information then need to be applied and evaluated to determine their effectiveness at answering the question or solving the problem. Finally, a reassessment of the answer or solution in light of the original question or problem needs to take place to make sure a suitable answer or solution has been generated.

These problem solving steps are nicely captured in the rubric (Figure 11.1) developed by Scott Benke and Kathy Buschman, math teachers at Josephinum Academy, a small Catholic college preparatory school for girls grades 6-12 in Chicago.

Figure 11.1: Rubric for Problem Solving

Problem-Solving Rubric

General Criteria	Specific Criteria	Absent or Incorrect	Partially Developed	Adequately Developed	Fully Developed
Understand the features of a problem (understands the question, restates problem in own words)	**1. Identify important information** **2. Represent understanding of problems verbally or in written form** **3. Determine missing information and identify what information is needed**	1. None of the important information is identified 2. Verbal/written representation of problem is inadequate/incomplete 3. Cannot determine whether or not information is missing	1. Not all of the important information is identified 2. Verbal/written representation of problem shows some signs of understanding 3. Can determine that information is missing, but cannot identify all of the information needed	1. Important information is identified 2. Represents an understanding of the problem verbally and in written form 3. Can determine whether or not information is missing and identify information needed	1. Clearly distinguishes relevant from irrelevant information 2. Precisely represents an understanding of the problem verbally and in written form 3. Can determine whether or not information is missing and can identify information needed
Explore problems (Draw diagram, construct a model/chart, records data, looks for patterns)	**1. Anticipate possible solutions** **2. Predict solutions to problems and provide rationales** **3. Determine potential strategies for solving problems**	1. Cannot anticipate possible solutions 2. No rationale provided 3. Cannot determine possible strategies to use	1. Cannot anticipate possible solutions 2. No rationale provided 3. Can only identify one potential strategy	1. Anticipates possible solutions 2. Rationale is incomplete or inaccurate 3. Determines potential strategies to solve problem	1. Anticipates possible solutions 2. Provides sound rationale 3. Determines potential strategies to solve the problem

Figure 11.1: Rubric for Problem Solving *(continued)*

Problem-Solving Rubric					
General Criteria	Specific Criteria	Absent or Incorrect	Partially Developed	Adequately Developed	Fully Developed
Select an appropriate strategy (guesses and checks, makes a list, solves a simpler problem, works backwards, estimates a solution)	1. Select strategies that seem most appropriate 2. Divide problem solving process into anticipated stages	1. Cannot determine appropriate strategies 2. Cannot divide problem into stages for solving	1. Selects inappropriate strategies 2. Attempts to but cannot or ineffectively divides problem into stages for solving	1. Selects strategy that seems appropriate, but may not be the most efficient 2. Divides problem into stages for solving	1. Selects strategies that are appropriate 2. Efficiently divides problem solving process into anticipated stages
Solve problems (implements a strategy with an accurate solution)	1. Monitor problem solving processes through each step 2. Complete necessary steps to solve the problem efficiently 3. Adjust uses of or select alternate strategies as necessary	1. Is unable to monitor problem solving processes 2. Is unable to complete any of the steps toward solving the problem 3. Is unable to adjust or select alternate strategies	1. Monitors problem solving processes through a portion of the steps 2. Completes some of the necessary steps to solve the problem 3. May show signs of adjusting strategies, and is not able to select an alternate strategy	1. Monitors problem solving processes through each step 2. Completes necessary steps to solve the problem, but not necessarily efficiently 3. Adjusts uses of strategy but is not able to select an alternate (and possibly more efficient) strategy	1. Monitors problem solving processes through each step 2. Completes necessary steps to solve the problem efficiently 3. Adjusts uses of or selects alternate strategies as necessary

Figure 11.1: Rubric for Problem Solving *(continued)*

		Problem-Solving Rubric			
General Criteria	Specific Criteria	Absent or Incorrect	Partially Developed	Adequately Developed	Fully Developed
Review, revise and extend problems (verify, explore, analyze, evaluate strategy or solution, formulate a rule)	1. Apply methods for checking work 2. Evaluate solution using methods chosen 3. Determine whether or not solution makes sense 4. Rework problem if solution is inaccurate	1. Does not attempt to check work 2. No evaluation of solution exists 3. Is unable to determine whether or not solution makes sense 4. Is unable to determine whether or not the solution is accurate	1. Attempts to check accuracy of work using incorrect method 2. Attempts to evaluate solution, although methods may be flawed 3. Is unable to determine whether or not solution makes sense 4. Is unable to determine whether or not the solution is accurate	1. Applies a correct method for checking work 2. Evaluates solution using a viable method for solving problem, although possibly inefficiently 3. Determines whether or not solution makes sense 4. Determines whether or not solution is accurate, but may have difficulty reworking the problem	1. Applies correct and efficient methods for checking work 2. Evaluates solution using accurate/ efficient methods 3. Determines whether or not solution makes sense 4. Determines whether or not solution is accurate and rework as necessary

The rubric intelligently fleshes out the general steps of problem solving into more specific elements of the process. The language of both, however, is written broadly enough to be applicable to any disciplinary problem solving.

A classroom teacher could follow the process I outlined earlier to begin developing one or more of these subskills of problem solving. But what is a library media specialist to do? Some of you already know the answer to that question because you have already found ways to contribute to the assessment program at your school. However, if that is not the case, you can recruit a teacher, team, or department to join in such a quest.

For your sanity and to make the adventure more attractive for your collaborators in assessment, emphasize that you want to start small. What might that look like for problem solving?

First, reach consensus on what is meant by problem solving. Emphasize a broader conception of it so it can be applied more universally. Use your expertise to suggest what these different steps can look like.

Second, select one or more of the subskills (e.g., define the problem) with which to begin. Although students typically will complete all the steps of problem solving whether they are solving a math problem, completing a research paper, or constructing a piece of art, you can *intentionally and explicitly highlight and target* certain of those steps. Once others (and you) see how one step can be targeted, developed, and assessed, it will be easier to add deliberate focus on the other steps down the road.

Third, work with the teacher, team, or department to design a brief summative assessment that adequately captures student application of the subskill(s).

Fourth, using the summative assessment as a guide, identify some specific places in the curriculum where these skills are relevant. If working with an elementary classroom teacher, select a unit or two that lend themselves to the subskill(s) of problem solving you are targeting. For example, Susan Dobrodt, LMC Director at Patterson Elementary School in Naperville, Illinois, created an excellent integrated, third-grade unit with accompanying assessments and rubrics (<http://jonathan.mueller.faculty.noctrl.edu/toolbox/examples/tasks_elementary_integrated.htm>) that easily could be adapted to teach and assess specific problem-solving skills.

If working with a middle school team, encourage them to consider where the subskill(s) best fits across math, language arts, science, social studies, technology, and so on. Can an integrated unit or research paper be targeted? If working with a high school music department, ask which processes or skills can best be conceptualized as problem solving, and how might the department craft language that describes a problem-solving subskill so it fits well across performance groups and classes.

Fifth, design some explicit opportunities for modeling and practice of the subskills. Here, the library media specialist can envision and suggest some brief exercises to embed within an already existing task or to serve as a standalone task, such as the types described earlier for practicing self-assessment (e.g., *apply the skill to own work, collaborate with peers, critique another's application of the skill, reflect on application*) or those described in Chapter 8 for information literacy skills.

Sixth, specifically check student work on at least a few of those tasks to formatively assess progress and as an occasion to provide feedback.

Finally, administer the summative assessment, preferably as part of the class or team's regular assessment package. To close the loop, review student performance on the assessment to inform future instruction.

Perhaps all of this cannot be implemented in one year. That is fine. *Proceed at a manageable pace.* Once you become comfortable with this process it becomes much easier to expand it. So, do not hesitate to start very, *very* small.

STEALTH ASSESSMENT

For those of you who do not feel as welcome to participate in the curriculum and assessment discussions at your school, or are unclear on how you might contribute, let me suggest a couple of approaches.

Using the knowledge gained from this text, design your own brief assessment that could be easily administered in the media center or wherever you meet students. Collect some data on what you consider a valuable skill or one that is often mentioned in your school but not regularly assessed. Share that assessment and data with those who you think might be interested in pursuing the assessment further. It does not have to be a full blown assessment. For example, just administer a couple of the tasks mentioned in Chapter 8 to gather a little data on some facet of students' information literacy skills. Real data are a good conversation starter.

Alternatively, connect with a teacher, team, or department and offer to create a few small tasks that students could complete, perhaps even in the media center, that addresses a critical skill. Again, beginning with something concrete helps move such conversations along. So, if you are aware of a particular skill, such as problem solving, that a teacher values, design a couple tasks *before* you meet with the teacher (or administrator). Many teachers will appreciate seeing such examples. Help with creating a rubric to evaluate student performance on such tasks may be even more appreciated.

FINAL THOUGHTS

Let me end by starting at the beginning. I have argued that developing a set of critical skills in our students will best prepare them for school, work, and life. If you agree, select a skill that you as a teacher, library media specialist, school, or district value; construct a meaningful assessment of that skill; design opportunities for students to practice it; check their understanding along the way; and work towards helping your students provide evidence on your assessment so they can apply the skill in authentic contexts. Good luck!

References

Alexander, P. A., Graham, S., & Harris, K. R. (1998). A perspective on strategy research: Progress and prospects. *Educational Psychology Review, 10*, 129-153.

American Library Association Presidential Committee on Information Literacy. (1989). *Final report*. Chicago: Author.

Association of American Colleges and Universities. (2002). *Greater expectations*. Retrieved February 8, 2008, from <http://www. greaterexpectations.org.>

Avery, E. F. (2003). *Assessing student learning outcomes for information literacy instruction in academic institutions*. Chicago: Association of College and Research Libraries.

Bahrick, H. P., & Hall, L. K. (2005). The importance of retrieval failures to long-term retention: A metacognitive explanation of the spacing effect. *Journal of Memory and Language, 52*, 566-577.

Baumeister, R. F., Bratslavsky, E., Muraven, M., & Tice, D. M. (1998). Ego depletion: Is the active self a limited resource? *Journal of Personality and Social Psychology, 74*, 1252-1265.

Bensley, D. A. (2006). Why great thinkers sometimes fail to think critically. *Skeptical Inquirer, 30*, 47-52.

Bereiter, C. (1995). A dispositional view of transfer. In A. McKeough, J. Lupart, & A. Marini (Eds.), *Teaching for transfer: Fostering generalization in learning* (pp. 21-34). New Jersey: Lawrence Erlbaum.

Black, P., & Wiliam, D. (1998). Assessment and classroom learning. *Assessment in Education, 5*, 7-74.

Bloom, B., Englehart, M. Furst, E., Hill, W., & Krathwohl, D. (1956). *Taxonomy of educational objectives: The classification of educational goals. Handbook I: Cognitive domain*. New York: Longman.

Bransford, J. D., & Vye, N. (1989). A perspective on cognitive research and its implications for instruction. In L.B. Resnick & L.E. Klopfer (Eds.), *Toward the thinking curriculum: Current cognitive research* (1989 Yearbook of the Association for Supervision and Curriculum Development). Alexandria, VA:

Association for Supervision and Curriculum Development.

Bridgeland, J. M., DiIulio, Jr., J. J., & Morison, K. B. (2006). *The silent epidemic: Perspectives of high school dropouts.* Bill & Melinda Gates Foundation, Peter D. Hart Research Associates.

Bruffee, K. (1995). Sharing our toys: Cooperative learning versus collaborative learning. *Change, Jan/Feb*, 12-18.

Campbell, J. I. D., & Graham, D. J. (1985). Mental multiplication skill: Structure, process, and acquisition. *Canadian Journal of Psychology, 39*, 338-366.

Chappuis, S., & Chappuis, J. (2007/2008). The best value in formative assessment. *Educational Leadership, 65*, 14-18.

Collison, J. (1992). Using performance assessment to determine mathematical dispositions. *Arithmetic Teacher, Feb.*, 40-47.

Common Core of Learning Committee. (1987). *Connecticut's Common Core of Learning.* Hartford, CT: Connecticut State Board of Education.

Dempster, F. N. (1988). Retroactive interference in the retention of prose: A reconsideration and new evidence. *Applied Cognitive Psychology, 2*, 97-113.

Dempster, F. N. (1989). Spacing effects and their implications for theory and practice. *Educational Psychology Review, 1*, 309–330.

Dempster, F. N. (1993). Exposing our students to less should help them learn more. *Phi Delta Kappan, 74*, 432-437.

Dunning, D., Johnson, K. L., Ehrlinger, J., & Kruger, J. (2003). Why people fail to recognize their own incompetence. *Current Directions in Psychological Science, 12*, 83-87.

Dweck, C. S. (1999). Caution-praise can be dangerous. *American Educator, 23*, 4-9.

Dweck, C. S. (2006). *Mindset: The new psychology of success.* New York: Random House.

Dweck, C. S., & Molden, D. C. (2005). Self-theories: Their impact on competence motivation and acquisition. In A. J. Elliot & C. S. Dweck (Eds.), *Handbook of competence and motivation* (pp. 122-140). New York: The Guilford Press.

Ellis, A. K. (2001). Cooperative learning. In A. K. Ellis (Ed.), *Research on educational innovations.* Larchmont, NY: Eye on Education.

Fink, A. (2002). *How to sample in surveys* (2nd ed.). Thousand Oaks, CA: Sage.

Fisher, D., Grant, M., Frey, N., & Johnson, C. (2007/2008). Taking formative assessment school-wide. *Educational Leadership, 65*, 64-68.

Flavell, J. H. (1971). First discussant's comments: What is memory development the development of? *Human Development, 14*, 272-278.

Flavell, J. H. (1979). Metacognition and cognitive monitoring: A new area of cognitive-developmental inquiry. *American Psychologist, 34*, 906-911.

Forman, G., & Kuschner, D. (1977). *The child's construction of knowledge.*

Belmont, CA: Wadworth Co.

Galles, G. M. (1987). Schools already teach too much. October 26, 1987. *Chicago Tribune.*

Gates, W. (2005). What's wrong with American high schools. March 4, 2005. *Chicago Tribune.*

Haladyna, T. M. (1999). *Developing and validating multiple-choice test items.* Mahwah, NJ: Lawrence Erlbaum Associates.

Harada, V. H., & Yoshina, J. M. (2005). *Assessing learning: Librarians and teachers as partners.* Westport, CT: Libraries Unlimited.

Hattie, J., Biggs, J., & Purdie, N. (1996). Effects of learning skills interventions on student learning: A meta-analysis. *Review of Educational Research, 66,* 99-136.

Herman, J. L., Aschbacher, P. R., & Winters, L. (1992). *A practical guide to alternative assessment.* Alexandria, VA: ASCD.

Johnson, D. W., & Johnson, F. (1991). *Joining together: Group theory and group skills* (4th ed.). Englewood Cliffs, NJ: Prentice Hall.

Johnson, D. W., & Johnson, R. T. (1994). *Learning together and alone: Cooperative, competitive, and individualistic learning* (4th ed.). Boston: Allyn and Bacon.

Karoly, L., & Panis, C. W. A. (2004). *The 21st century at work: Forces shaping the future workforce and workplace in the United States.* Santa Monica, CA: RAND Corporation.

Kluger, A. N., & DeNisi, A. (1996). The effects of feedback interventions on performance: A historical review, a meta-analysis, and preliminary feedback theory. *Psychological Bulletin, 119,* 254-284.

Kuklinski, M. R., & Weinstein, R. S. (2001). Classroom and developmental differences in a path model of teacher expectancy effects. *Child Development, 72,* 1554-1578.

Kulik, J. A., & Kulik, C. L. C. (1988). Timing of feedback and verbal learning. *Review of Educational Research, 58,* 79-97.

Locke, E. A. & Latham, G. P. (2002). Building a practically useful theory of goal setting and task motivation. *American Psychologist, 57,* 705-717.

Maki, R. H., & Berry, S. L. (1984). Meta-comprehension of text material. *Journal of Experimental Psychology: Learning, Memory, and Cognition, 10,* 663-679.

Marzano, R. J., Pickering, D., & McTighe, J. (1993). *Assessing student outcomes: Performance assessment using the Dimensions of Learning Model.* Alexandria, VA: ASCD.

Marzano, R. J. (2006). *Classroom assessment and grading that work.* Alexandria, VA: ASCD.

Mayer, R. E., & Wittrock, M. C. (1996). Problem-solving transfer. In R. Berliner & R. Calfee (Eds.), *Handbook of educational psychology* (pp. 47-62). New York: Macmillan.

Mueller, J. (2005). Authentic assessment in the classroom ... and the library media center. *Library Media Connection, April/May,* 14-18.

Mueller, J. (2006). Constructing good tests. In J. Mueller, *Authentic assessment toolbox*. Retrieved September 15, 2007, from <http://jonathan.mueller.faculty.noctrl.edu/toolbox/tests.htm>.

Muraven, M., Tice, D. M., & Baumeister, R. F. (1998). Self-control as limited resource: Regulatory depletion patterns. *Journal of Personality and Social Psychology, 74,* 774-789.

Myers, D. G. (2008). *Social psychology* (9th ed.). Boston: McGraw-Hill.

Neely, T. Y. (2006). *Information literacy assessment.* American Library Association: Chicago.

Neisser, U. (1967). *Cognitive psychology.* New York: Appleton-Century-Crofts.

Panitz, T. (1997). Collaborative versus cooperative learning: Comparing the two definitions helps understand the nature of interactive learning. *Cooperative Learning and College Teaching, 8,* 3-13.

Partnership for 21st Century Skills. (2006). *Results that matter: 21st century skills and high school reform.* Tucson, AZ: Author. Retrieved April 12, 2007, from <http://www.21stcenturyskills.org>.

Pashler, H., Zarow, G., & Triplett, B. (2003). Is temporal spacing of tests helpful even when it inflates error rates? *Journal of Experimental Psychology: Learning, Memory, and Cognition, 29,* 1051-1057.

Perkins, D., Jay, E., & Tishman, S. (1993). Beyond abilities: A dispositional theory of thinking. *Merrill-Palmer Quarterly, 39,* 1-21.

Pintrich, P. R., Wolters, C., & Baxter, G. (2000). Assessing metacognition and self-regulated learning. In G. Schraw & J. Impara (Eds.), *Issues in the measurement of metacognition* (pp. 43-97). Lincoln, NE: Buros Institute of Mental Measurements.

Popham, W. J. (1999). Why standardized tests don't measure educational quality. *Educational Leadership, 56,* 8-15.

Popham, W. J. (2005). All about accountability/instructional quality: Collecting credible evidence. *Educational Leadership, 62,* 80-81.

Pressley, M., & Yokoi, L. (1994). Motion for a new trial on transfer. *Educational Researcher, 23,* 36-38.

Ratzlaff, S., & Diercks, R. (1995). Student-teacher created visual rubrics: Models to guide and assess research projects. In *Assessment in action: Collaborative action research focused on mathematics and science assessments* (pp. 16-18). Denver, CO: McRel.

Roediger, H. L., & Karpicke, J. D. (2006). Test-enhanced learning: Taking memory tests improves long-term retention. *Psychological Science, 17,* 249-255.

Rosenthal, R. (2002). Covert communications in classrooms, clinics, courtrooms, and cubicles. *American Psychologist, 57,* 839–849.

Sadler, D.R. (1989). Formative assessment and the design of instructional systems. *Instructional Science, 18,* 119-144.

Schmidt, W. H., McKnight, C. C., & Raizen, S. A. (1996). *A splintered vision: An investigation of U.S. science and mathematics education, executive summary.* Michigan State University, Lansing, MI: National Research Center for the Third International Mathematics and Science Study. Retrieved October 15, 2006, from <http://ustimss.msu.edu/splintrd.pdf>.

Schmoker, M. J., & Marzano, R. J. (1999). Realizing the promise of standards-based education. *Educational Leadership, 56,* 17-21.

Sinkavich, F. J. (1995). Performance and meta-memory: Do students know what they don't know? *Instructional Psychology, 22,* 77-87.

Slavin, R. E. (2006). *Educational psychology: Theory and practice* (8th ed.). Boston: Allyn and Bacon.

Slavin, R. E., Hurley, E. A., & Chamberlain, A. (2003). Cooperative learning and achievement: Theory and research. In W. M. Reynolds & G. E. Miller (Eds.), *Handbook of psychology: Educational psychology, Vol. 7.* (pp. 177-198). Hoboken, NJ: John Wiley & Sons, Inc.

Steffe, L. P., & Gale, J. (Eds.). (1995). *Constructivism in education.* Hillsdale, NJ: Erlbaum.

Stiggins, R. J. (1987). "Design and Development of Performance Assessment." *Educational Measurement: Issues and Practices,* Fall: 33-42.

Wiggins, G. P. (1998). *Educative assessment: Designing assessments to inform and improve student performance.* San Francisco: Jossey-Bass Publishers.

Wiggins, G. P., & McTighe, J. (1998). *Understanding by design.* Alexandria, VA: ASCD.

Willingham, D. T. (2003). Students remember what they think about. *American Educator, 27,* 37-41.

Willingham, D. T. (2007). Critical thinking: Why is it so hard to teach? *American Educator, 31,* 8-19.

Wittrock, M. C. (1991). Testing and recent research in cognition. In M.C. Wittrock & E.L. Baker (Eds.), *Testing and cognition.* Englewood Cliffs: NJ: Prentice-Hall.

Zogby International Poll (2006). Retrieved October 12, 2006, from <http://www.zogby.com/wf-AOL%20National.pdf>.

Index

Authentic tasks, 21-22, 27, 30-32, 35, 39, 50, 63, 68, 99, 107, 109
Constructed-response tasks, 20-22, 48, 51, 53, 83, 95-96
Criteria, 8-9, 19, 27, 31-43, 46, 49-51, 55-57, 63-65, 67, 81-85, 88,
    105, 109, 114-117, 119-121
Descriptors, 36, 43, 49
Dispositions, 7, 10, 16, 116
Feedback, 8, 17-18, 22, 26, 49, 52, 54-56, 60, 71-75, 77, 88-89, 93,
    98-101, 104, 107, 109-110, 113, 116-117, 123
Forced-choice measures, 19, 79, 88, 107, 109
Formative assessment, 18-19, 25-26, 45-46, 51, 53-54, 57, 59, 61,
    67, 70-75, 77, 79, 88-89, 94, 99, 110-111, 113, 116-117, 123
Information literacy, 10-11, 15, 17, 24-25, 28, 46, 48-50, 57, 77-81,
    85-86, 88-89, 91, 95, 103-107, 110-111, 117, 123
Librarian/Library media specialist, 13, 16-18, 28, 55, 63, 71-72,
    77, 79, 86, 88, 95, 104-105, 110, 113, 117-118, 122-124
Metacognition, 60
No Child Left Behind (NCLB), 4, 18
Outcomes, 46, 78, 80
Performance tasks (see also Authentic tasks), 62, 79, 107, 109
Practice, 1-2, 11, 15-17, 26, 42, 45, 51-55, 57, 71, 73-75, 77,
    88-89, 99-101, 103-104, 110, 113-118, 123-124
Reflection, 2, 17-18, 29, 52, 56, 68-70, 72, 77, 88-89, 99-101,
    115-116
Rubrics
    Analytic, 35, 37, 39-41, 66, 109
    Holistic, 35, 39-41, 65-66
    Levels of performance, 35-39, 41-42, 56, 84
Skills
    Analytical, 8, 14
    Collaborative, 8, 11, 49, 91-101
    Communication, 8, 11, 15, 91-92
    Creative (innovative), 10
    Evaluation, 4, 8, 49-50, 63, 65, 85, 88
    Goal-setting, 9, 114
    Information literacy (see Information literacy)
    Integration, 9
    Interpersonal, 8, 92, 99
    Leadership, 8, 45
    Logic/reasoning, 8, 15
    Metacognitive, 1, 3, 9, 11, 13, 15, 17, 45, 59-62, 70, 77
    Monitoring (progress/performance), 4, 9, 14, 42, 46, 57,
        59-75, 77
    Problem-solving, 7, 9-11, 15, 17
    Quantitative reasoning, 8, 15
    Self-assessment, 9, 13, 42, 57, 75, 98, 113-114, 116-117